ENTANGLED ALLIES

ENTANGLED ALLIES

U.S. Policy Toward Greece, Turkey, and Cyprus

Monteagle Stearns

COUNCIL ON FOREIGN RELATIONS PRESS

NEW YORK

COUNCIL ON FOREIGN RELATIONS BOOKS

The Council on Foreign Relations, Inc., is a nonprofit and nonpartisan organization devoted to promoting improved understanding of international affairs through the free exchange of ideas. The Council does not take any position on questions of foreign policy and has no affiliation with, and receives no funding from, the United States government.

From time to time, books and monographs written by members of the Council's research staff or visiting fellows, or commissioned by the Council, or written by an independent author with critical review contributed by a Council study or working group are published with the designation "Council on Foreign Relations Book." Any book or monograph bearing that designation is, in the judgment of the Committee on Studies of the Council's Board of Directors, a responsible treatment of a significant international topic worthy of presentation to the public. All statements of fact and expressions of opinion contained in Council books are, however, the sole responsibility of the author.

If you would like more information on Council publications, please write the Council on Foreign Relations, 58 East 68th Street, New York, NY 10021, or call the Publications Office at (212) 734-0400.

Library of Congress Cataloguing-in-Publication Data

Stearns, Monteagle, 1924–
    Entangled allies : U.S. policy toward Greece, Turkey, and Cyprus / Monteagle Stearns.
        p.   cm.
    Includes bibliographical references and index.
    ISBN 0-87609-110-9 : $16.95
    1. Mediterranean Region—Foreign relations—United States. 2. United States—Foreign relations—Mediterranean Region. 3. Mediterranean Region—Foreign relations—1945– 4. United States—Foreign relations—1945– I. Title.

DE85.5.U6S74   1992   91-41142
327.7301822—dc20   CIP

Cover Design: Whit Vye

For Toni

CONTENTS

LIST OF MAPS

PREFACE

This study expresses views about the management of U.S. foreign policy and, specifically, about the management of our Aegean and Cyprus policies that grew out of my experience as a professional diplomat who served almost half of my career—fifteen years—working on the interrelated problems of Greece, Turkey, and Cyprus. In that time, I accumulated the usual frustrations that dog diplomats (and soldiers) as they try to catch, and then hold, the attention of their distracted governments. From this standpoint, the study can be said to have had a cathartic effect on me, just as it offers me a welcome opportunity to explain to a wider audience why I believe the relationships of Greece, Turkey, and Cyprus are not as hopelessly snarled as they seem, and how the United States, with more imaginative diplomacy and greater attention to political realities in the region, can help disentangle them.

The book is divided into ten chapters, with an introduction to establish the scene for readers who are not specialists in the worlds of Byzantine and Ottoman state politics, as practiced in the latter half of the twentieth century. The first three chapters deal with various aspects of U.S. policy in the area since the Truman Doctrine; the next three with Soviet and NATO policies, Greece, Turkey, and Cyprus in relation to the Middle East, and finally in relation to each other; the three following chapters analyze Greek-Turkish-Cypriot differences and suggest the most promising lines of approach if they are to be resolved; and the concluding chapter advances reasons for a new diplomatic initiative at this time and suggests the appropriate role for the United States. I should add that I owe the book's title, and much else, to my wife, Toni, to whom it is fondly dedicated.

Support and assistance in completing this study, which I began in 1987, while still in the Department of State, have been extended by many people, first and foremost by the Council on

Foreign Relations and its president, Peter Tarnoff, and by its director of studies, my friend, Nicholas X. Rizopoulos, who not only brought me to the Council as Whitney H. Shepardson Fellow and shared the rigors and pleasures of an extended trip to the region in the summer of 1990 but has been a matchless source of informed comment and criticism since the process of composition began. Many members of the Council staff have given the project valuable time and thought. Carol Rath, in particular, has worked skillfully over many months to help me complete the manuscript.

I owe a special debt of thanks to Rita E. Hauser, whose generous support for the Council's Project in Regional Conflict enabled me to benefit intellectually from a series of three seminars devoted to particular portions of my manuscript, and to Adm. Stansfield Turner, whom I first met in 1974 when he was dealing with the problems of NATO's southeastern flank from his CINCSOUTH headquarters in Naples, for taking the time to chair these seminars and for his thoughtful and perceptive comments on the issues discussed. Linda Wrigley's work as seminar rapporteur and her later editing of the manuscript assured that many good ideas expressed in the seminars were not lost and also that they were incorporated into the manuscript.

All of the many seminar participants helped me to sharpen the focus of my presentation on some aspect of Greek-Turkish-Cypriot relations. The presence at one or more of the seminars of former secretary of state Cyrus R. Vance and former State Department counselor Matthew Nimetz added immeasurably to their value, as did the participation in the final seminar of Professor Duygu Bazoglue Sezer of Bilkent University in Ankara, whose contributions to the study of Turkish-Greek relations have been extensive, dispassionate, and important. I would also like to thank those who went to the trouble of sending me written comments: Professors Tozun Bahcheli of King's College in Ontario, Van Coufoudakis of Indiana University at Fort Wayne, John O. Iatrides of Southern Connecticut State University, Victor Papacosma of Kent State University, Harry Psomiades of Queens College, and Birol Yesilada of the University of Missouri-Columbia; Fred Haynes, president of the American

Friends of Turkey; and Seymour J. Rubin, senior consultant to the American Society of International Law.

I want also to express my gratitude to the Woodrow Wilson International Center for Scholars, which awarded me a fellowship in the academic year 1987–1988, enabling me to devote a sustained period of time to research, discussion, and composition in the wonderful environment of the Smithsonian castle, which combines, in just the right proportion, the seclusion needed to develop ideas and the challenge needed to test them. Deputy Director Samuel F. Wells, Jr. and Robert S. Litwak, director of the International Security Studies Program, assisted me generously and wisely throughout my ten months there to make the best use of my time and of the Center's remarkable resources. I wish also to express heartfelt thanks to my research assistant, Contantine Symeonides-Tsatsos, for his imaginative and indefatigable help in bringing to my attention valuable source material in the Library of Congress and sharing with me his own insights on Greek foreign policy. My Turkish Cypriot research assistant, Selen Sertug, was especially helpful in reviewing and summarizing the Turkish newspaper archives of the Library of Congress. Of many outstanding fellows at the Center I would like to single out Professor Dimitri Constas of the Panteios University of Social and Political Sciences in Athens for comments that helped refine my thinking on specific portions of the manuscript.

The Council's director of studies and I wish jointly to express our appreciation to the U.S. embassies in Ankara, Nicosia, and Athens, and to the staff of the Commander in Chief, Allied Forces, Southern Europe, in Naples, especially to the political advisor, Stephen P. Dawkins, for the assistance and hospitality they extended to us in a busy period. We also wish to thank for their participation in Council seminars and for more informal exchanges in Washington: Ambassador Nelson Ledsky, the State Department's Special Cyprus Coordinator; David Ransom, director of the Office of Southern European Affairs (EUR/SE), and his predecessor, Ambassador Townsend Friedman; Susan Kempe, Officer in Charge of Cyprus Affairs, and other members of the staff of EUR/SE. Ellen Laipson of the National Intelligence Council, the author of many informative studies on Greece, Turkey, and Cyprus when she was serving in the Congressional Research Service of the Library of Congress, also was a stimulating and knowledgeable interlocutor. My old colleague, George Bader, of the Office of International Security Policy in the Department of Defense, corrected some of my statistical data but bears no responsibility for errors if they remain. Katherine Wilkins, of Chairman Lee Hamilton's House Subcommittee on Europe and the Middle East, was especially helpful in setting forth congressional concerns affecting Greece and Turkey.

This study began in the Foreign Service Institute's Center for the Study of Foreign Affairs, whose then director, Hans Binnendikj (now director of Georgetown University's Institute for the Study of Diplomacy), provided me with the support necessary to begin my research, as well as indispensable advice in carrying it forward.

Since moving to the Boston area three years ago, I have been fortunate to maintain ties with Harvard University's Center for International Affairs and Center for European Studies. Samuel P. Huntington of the former and Stanley Hoffmann of the latter have enabled me to participate in and profit from various programs and activities that have contributed significantly to my work. I wish also to thank Professor Theodore A. Couloumbis of Athens University for his encouragement and for making available to me his excellent, but, alas, now out of print, study of U.S. policy in the region, *The United States, Greece and Turkey: The Troubled Triangle*, published by Praeger in 1983.

Last, I would like to express appreciation for her services in preparing the Cyprus chapter of this manuscript to Fern Kurland, my secretary in the International Relations Department of Simmons College, where I had the pleasure of serving as Warburg Professor from 1988 to 1990.

In his preface to the first edition of *Russia in Flux* in 1941, Sir John Maynard declared that he had "sought to banish from these pages wolves, angels, and predatory fat gentlemen with a gift for arithmetic." Trying to write objectively about Greece, Turkey, and Cyprus presents similar problems, but, in the same spirit, I have tried to banish from these pages rascally Greeks,

predatory Turks, and sharp-eyed Cypriots with a gift for exploiting the weaknesses of both. If my most pointed criticisms are
reserved for U.S. policy, it is because this is the policy I know best,
not because I do not think there is enough blame to go around.
In any event, the opinions and points of emphasis in this volume
are my own, as are the conclusions and recommendations. Those
who were good enough to discuss them with me, either to agree
or to disagree, bear no responsibility for the form they have
finally assumed.

The Mediterranean Basin

Ascherl

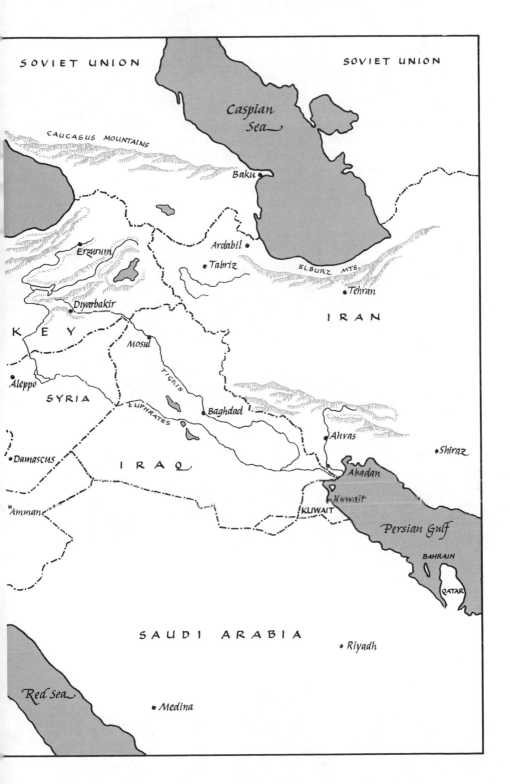

INTRODUCTION

If U.S. foreign policy before World War II had been inspired by prophets and informed by sacred texts, the prophets would have been George Washington and Henry Ford, and the texts would have read "avoid entangling alliances" and "history is bunk." The post–World War II foreign policy of the United States seems, at first glance, a complete repudiation of these precepts—especially so in the case of Greece and Turkey, with which the United States became closely associated under the Truman Doctrine in 1947, more than two years before the creation of the North Atlantic Treaty Organization (NATO), and with which we continue to conduct an often tempestuous relationship that is affected at least as much by history as by statecraft.

A closer look at U.S. foreign policy since World War II, including notably our policy in the Persian Gulf crisis of 1990–1991, suggests that the U.S. attitude toward diplomatic entanglements and the uses of history has not changed so drastically. We continue to be better at military than diplomatic planning and more sensitive to headlines than to history. Our political leaders may cite the lessons of history more than their predecessors, but when they do, they are usually marshaling arguments to support a foreign policy initiative already taken for other reasons. More often than not, the lesson in any case is a negative one—to avoid another Munich or another Vietnam—and the promise is that we will not get bogged down, which are the post-Vietnam code words for not getting entangled. As we shall see, this predilection for qualified engagement has shaped in a particular way our long-standing relationship with Greece, Turkey, and Cyprus.

Anticipating his first summit meeting with Soviet president Mikhail S. Gorbachev—held in December 1989 off Valletta, the capital of the Mediterranean island state of Malta—President George Bush was moved by Ozymandian images of dead em-

1

pires to see in their passing a reminder that the security of nations depends not on domination but on trust.

"When we meet," he said, "we will be on ships at anchor in a Mediterranean bay that has served as a sea-lane of commerce and conflict for more than 2,000 years. This ancient port has been conquered by Caesar and sultan, crusader and king. Its forts and watchtowers survey a sea that entombs the scuttled ships of empires lost—slave galleys, galleons, dreadnoughts, destroyers. These ships, once meant to guard lasting empires, now litter the ocean floor and guard nothing more than reefs of coral."[1]

The president might have added that the Mediterranean, since antiquity, has been swept by strong and perverse winds, which scuttled as many galleys and galleons as were lost in combat and which nearly scuttled the summit meeting. He might also have noted that the Mediterranean today, although free of the dominion of empires, is as tormented as ever by absence of trust.

Nowhere is this more evident than in the relations of the three eastern Mediterranean states—Greece, Turkey, and Cyprus—that provide the focus for this book. The first two have been warring rivals since the Middle Ages and distrustful allies since their admission to NATO in 1952; for almost as long, the third, independent since 1960, has been a bone of contention between them, occupied by the Turks as early as 1571 and as late as 1974.

While the role of the United States in the Mediterranean after World War II has not been exactly imperial, it has certainly been hegemonic. The U.S. Sixth Fleet has been the dominant seapower in the Mediterranean since 1946; it was introduced into the eastern Mediterranean a year later, in 1947, mainly to demonstrate military support for Greece and Turkey, in whose security the United States had declared a special interest in March through the Truman Doctrine.

Such a long-standing security relationship might have been expected to cultivate in its beneficiaries sufficient trust to assure smooth relations among them. Greece and Turkey, after all, were relieved of their sense of insecurity in the face of postwar Soviet policy; Cyprus exchanged its status as a British Crown colony for independence; the United States was granted the use of military bases in Greece and Turkey—and of the British sovereign base areas in Cyprus—and, in recognition of the obligations of mutual security, extended generous military assistance to the former and economic assistance to all three.

The relations of the United States with Greece, Turkey, and Cyprus have not been smooth, however, and are animated by less trust today than in 1947. Cyprus is a divided state, with Turkish troops occupying the north of the island; Greek and Turkish differences over the Aegean shelf, territorial sea and air space, military command-and-control arrangements, and the interpretation of existing treaties are more inflamed than ever and have six times brought the two allies to the verge of war since joining NATO; and the United States has seen its security relationship with Greece and Turkey become, over time, less a source of mutual reassurance than of mutual recrimination.

It is the purpose of this book to examine how such brave beginnings produced so unsatisfactory a state of current affairs. One of its theses is that U.S. policy toward Greece, Turkey, and Cyprus has in the past been so exclusively devoted to the containment of Soviet influence in the Aegean and eastern Mediterranean that we have learned little about the countries that did the containing and have generally minimized or disregarded their own foreign policy concerns when they did not coincide with ours. As in other parts of the world, when the United States has regarded the problems of Greece, Turkey, and Cyprus it has been unable to see the trees for the forest until one of them caught fire.

The reluctance of the United States and NATO to be distracted from their principal mission of Soviet containment by political differences within the alliance, like those between Greece and Turkey, was no more than the conventional attitude of alliances formed to deter or defeat a common antagonist. What we know of the Delian League in the fifth century B.C., suggests that Athens was just as disinclined to take its eye from the Persian threat as Washington was from the Soviet. The price paid by Athens for its strategic preoccupation with Persia was the unraveling of its alliance system and eventual defeat by its former ally, Sparta. The price of Washington's neglect of Greek-

Turkish differences was the steady weakening of NATO's defensive capability in an area, the Aegean, where its vital interests converged with those of the Warsaw Pact. Long before the decline and fall of the Soviet alliance system, the vulnerabilities of NATO's southeastern flank were clear. If the central front of NATO in Germany represented the military heart of the alliance, its Achilles' heel was assuredly located where Homer placed his wounded hero, in the Aegean waters of the southeastern sector. That the Soviets proved incapable of taking advantage of these vulnerabilities says more about their weakness than NATO's strength.

The author of this study is not a revisionist and, on the subject of Soviet expansionism, believes that we may have exaggerated the threat but certainly did not invent or provoke it. Stalin's Soviet Union, even in the retrospect of decades, still looks like a menacing and paranoid neighbor, as the Greeks, the Turks, and we ourselves saw it at the time of the Truman Doctrine. For all the limitations and occasional obtuseness of U.S. policy in the region, it was successful. Few Greeks, and even fewer Turks, believe they would be better off if they had gone the way of the Bulgarians or Yugoslavs. But a U.S. policy that was, on balance, successful in achieving its main objective in the past is not necessarily sufficient to the demands of the future, especially to the demands of a future in which our ability to address new and threatening global issues is impaired by older regional problems that we neglected in the past. In a world of shrinking natural resources, riven by ethnic and religious disputes, where the easiest technology to transfer is military technology and where petty tyrants can accordingly amass huge arsenals, no problem between states is insignificant, and no burning tree fails potentially to endanger the forest.

These are the practical, policy-oriented reasons for reexamining U.S. policy toward Greece, Turkey, and Cyprus. There are other reasons as well. The way the United States has handled its relations with these three countries reveals a great deal about the U.S. diplomatic method, about the way we visualize our leadership of the Western world and the way we exercise it. Greece and Turkey, partly because of what they are and partly because of where they are, have regularly stimulated in the U.S. foreign policy process all the contradictions, ambivalence, and tensions to which we are constitutionally and structurally vulnerable: between moral and practical considerations, between the desire for isolation and the fear of it, between military needs and political costs, between Congress and the executive. No region, except perhaps the Middle East and Indochina, has provoked more contention between internal political and external security factors in the development of U.S. foreign policy, and in neither the Middle East nor Indochina were we weighing the competing claims of military allies.

Greece and Turkey are our most remote NATO allies; despite the intimacy of our relations since 1947, our prior relationship was superficial, leaving little foundation of shared interest and understanding to cushion the shocks to which intimate relations can be more susceptible than casual ones. Over the same period unresolved Greek-Turkish problems have erupted in a series of crises—in Istanbul in 1955, in Cyprus in 1963, 1964, 1967, and 1974, and in the Aegean, where Greek-Turkish confrontations have been too numerous to mention but serious enough to threaten general hostilities as recently as 1987—that forced diplomatic choices on the United States it was reluctant to make. The result has been acute strain on the relations of all the states directly or indirectly affected, particularly those of Greece and Turkey with the United States and NATO.

The membership of Greece and Turkey in a common alliance has unquestionably helped to limit the scale of their military clashes. Curiously, however, it has done little to facilitate their diplomatic accommodation. Instead of enabling them to reconcile their differences by direct negotiation, their common alliance with the United States and Western Europe often appears to act as an impediment. Bilateral disputes acquire a multilateral dimension, and Athens and Ankara sometimes seem to be too busy protecting their respective positions in Washington and Brussels to pay serious attention to resolving the disputes themselves. The situation has been aggravated by an American diplomacy narrow in focus and better at reacting to events than anticipating them. U.S. interests in the eastern Mediterranean being primarily strategic and our ability to protect them primarily dependent on military facilities' agreements that we negotiate periodically with host governments which change, like our own, and which, like our own, have changing political agendas, U.S. policies in the area have often exhibited the faults of a single-track approach that is also episodic and inconsistent. It is small wonder that Greek prime ministers of very different political persuasions, Constantine Karamanlis and Andreas Papandreou, have both observed that one of the chief benefits to be gained from Greek-Turkish détente would be to break the habit both countries have acquired of trying to conduct their bilateral relations through Washington—the cumbersome "triangular relationship" that has been as galling to the Turks as to the Greeks. This awkward, three-sided relationship in turn produced the 7 : 10 ratio that Greece and its American supporters maintain must govern U.S. military assistance to Greece and Turkey and that has bedeviled the relations of successive U.S. administrations with both countries, not to mention Congress, since February 1975. This issue is discussed in detail in chapter 3, but we may note in passing that there is a certain irony in the fact that, although all subsequent U.S. administrations have complained that it was unrealistic to establish military aid levels by means of an arbitrary formula, the 7 : 10 ratio is probably the logical outcome of U.S. policies toward Greece and Turkey that have treated these countries more as factors in a geostrategic equation than as products of their own historical experience. Starting with the parallel letters addressed by Secretary of State John Foster Dulles to the Greek and Turkish prime ministers in 1955, and continuing with President Lyndon B. Johnson's stern rebuke to the Turkish prime minister in 1964, both of which episodes are examined in chapter 2, we have consistently behaved as though Greece and Turkey erased a millennium of their history when they signed the North Atlantic Treaty in February 1952, abandoning forever those national interests and objectives that were incompatible with U.S. efforts to maintain a balance of power with the Soviet Union. So mechanical and unreflective a policy was almost certain to produce mechanical and unreflective responses like the 7 : 10 ratio, as well as the kind of resentment and misunderstanding that have regrettably become characteristic of our relations with both countries.

We like to approach diplomacy as though it were engineering—a matter of building structures and edifices, alliances and bases, which will be serviceable in all climates and adaptable to all terrains. When the climate and terrain are favorable, U.S. foreign policy is durable and produces tangible benefits. When unfavorable, as in China after World War II, Southeast Asia twenty years later, and Iran in the late 1970s, U.S. foreign policy does not so much fail as collapse. In the years ahead, with a need to economize at home and abroad, we will be able to afford fewer collapses. The terrain and climate for structures that have endured, like NATO, will require closer attention, especially in areas where important U.S. interests exist and are best served by a stable strategic environment. The region of the eastern Mediterranean is one of these.

This is, therefore, an appropriate moment to take a fresh look at U.S. policy toward Greece, Turkey, and Cyprus. In doing so, the author assumes that the security nexus—as the Persian Gulf crisis amply demonstrated—will continue to be an important consideration for U.S. policymakers but that it will need more than a military rationale to make it endure in vastly different world conditions. Specifically, the political and economic dimensions of U.S. policy will need to be strengthened, and the United States must begin to take more seriously than it has in the past the plight of its divided NATO allies and of the divided Republic of Cyprus.

1

U.S. POLICY: THE CONTAINMENT OF GREECE, TURKEY, AND CYPRUS

Since March 1947, when the Truman Doctrine announced a new era in U.S. relations with Greece and Turkey, the U.S. government has betrayed uncertainty about where these two states should logically be situated in the spectrum of our relations with the rest of the world. They have never fitted comfortably into the global maps with which we were most familiar.

As late as the spring of 1974, for example, 22 years after they joined NATO, Greece and Turkey had still not joined the European bureau of the State Department. They remained instead the responsibility of State's Bureau of Near Eastern and South Asian Affairs (known as NEA, although the "A" stood for Africa until 1958, when a separate African bureau was created). For much of that period, the Greek and Turkish desks belonged to the Office of Greek, Turkish and Iranian Affairs (whose acronym was GTI). These three countries had little in common except their ancient hostilities, a modern history of internal instability, and their proximity to the Soviet bloc. Greece and Turkey were the southeastern flank of NATO and Turkey and Iran were the "northern tier" of the short-lived CENTO alliance (the Central Treaty Organization, created in 1955, and eventually comprising Britain, Iraq, Iran, Pakistan, and Turkey).[1] They were, in short, three countries as strategically important as they were bureaucratically marginal.

One unintentional effect of this grouping was to reinforce the State Department's inherent preference for bilateral over multilateral diplomacy. Among Foreign Service officers assigned to GTI there were numerous specialists in Greek or Turkish affairs but few with firsthand knowledge of both countries, much less of both languages and cultures. Even rarer was an NEA assistant secretary of state who had more than a cursory acquaintance with either country. Several assistant secretaries went on to serve as ambassadors to Greece or Turkey—George McGhee and Parker T. Hart to Turkey and George V. Allen and Phillips Talbot to Greece—but no one made the trip the other way. Furthermore, with the exception of the period immediately before and after the promulgation of the Truman Doctrine, the attention of the U.S. government, and hence of the assistant secretary of state, was virtually monopolized by the unending crisis in Arab-Israel relations. There was little time or incentive for senior officials to learn about relations between Greece and Turkey, whose principal foreign policy objectives, it was assumed, had been achieved with their admission to NATO. It was inconceivable to the U.S. government that two states which felt themselves directly threatened by the Soviet Union, which had insistently sought the protection of NATO membership, and which were receiving large amounts of military and economic aid from the United States would permit bilateral problems to get out of hand. Even in the small and chronically overworked Office of Greek, Turkish and Iranian Affairs, the patient requiring emergency treatment was usually Iran, first in 1946, when it became the focus of East-West tension over the presence of Soviet troops in Iranian Azerbaijan, then with the oil crisis of 1951–1953.[2]

If Greece and Turkey were stepchildren of the Bureau of Near Eastern and South Asian Affairs, they often were treated like orphans in the Bureau of European Affairs (EUR), which they at last joined in the summer of 1974. Twenty days before Turkish troops landed in Cyprus on July 20, Secretary of State Henry A. Kissinger, unfriendly to the policy recommendations he was receiving from NEA, abruptly transferred responsibility for Greek, Turkish, and Cypriot affairs to EUR, saddling a new assistant secretary and his deputy for southern Europe with a crisis involving countries they knew even less about than their predecessors in NEA. While there were many other reasons for U.S. indecisiveness in the summer of 1974—not least the paralysis of the presidency induced by Watergate and the imminent resignation of President Richard M. Nixon—it is beyond doubt that EUR, trying to orient itself in unfamiliar terrain, was less inclined to recommend bold initiatives, and perhaps also less concerned about lost opportunities, than NEA, with a longer institutional memory and greater familiarity with the problems, would have been.

Ten years later, Greek, Turkish, and Cypriot affairs still looked like an unwelcome burden to EUR, which remained preoccupied with the problems of the central European front. From 1982 until 1985, there was no deputy assistant secretary in EUR who was specifically responsible for Greece, Turkey, and Cyprus. The area was handled by a more junior officer designated the "deputy for policy." Bureaucratic distinctions rarely in themselves mold policy. They do, however, unerringly reflect the priorities of policymakers and, accordingly, the amount of policy-level attention a given area or problem is apt to receive. Although the deputy for policy was capable and energetic and enjoyed the undoubted confidence of his superiors, his title, like his cramped office a floor below the assistant secretary and his senior deputies, was a sure indication that the Reagan administration's State Department was planning no major moves in the area of Greek, Turkish, and Cypriot affairs. This proved to be the case, even though bureaucratic anomalies were removed in 1985 with the appointment of a full deputy assistant secretary responsible for Greece, Turkey, and Cyprus.

Admittedly, bold diplomacy was not a hallmark of the Reagan administration anywhere, except perhaps in relations with the Soviet Union in its final two years. Previous administrations did launch high-profile initiatives to address Greek-Turkish differences over the Aegean and Cyprus: The parallel letters sent by Secretary of State Dulles to the prime ministers of Greece and Turkey in 1955; the mission of Under Secretary of State George W. Ball to Greece, Turkey, and Cyprus, the development of the Acheson Plan, and the transmission of President Johnson's letter of warning to Turkish Prime Minister Ismet Inönü, all in 1964; the Vance mission in 1967; the Sisco mission in 1974; the Clifford mission in 1977; and the Cyprus proposals of State Department counselor Matthew Nimetz in 1978. Are these not indications that the United States has taken Greek-Turkish problems seriously and been willing to expend diplomatic capital to help resolve them?

The answer is "yes and no." All of the initiatives listed above, with the possible exception of the Nimetz proposals,[3] were launched as firefighting operations designed primarily to prevent general hostilities between Greece and Turkey or secure other short-term objectives, and only secondarily to resolve underlying differences. They represent the U.S. government's reaction to events that had already reached crisis proportions. More consistent attention at senior levels of the government, and a steadier hand at the working level, might have averted these crises altogether or, if this proved impossible, at least equipped U.S. officials with greater experience and a more delicate touch when they erupted. As it was, senior U.S. officials unfamiliar with the region were called on to deal with complicated and highly charged conflicts where the margin for decision was already narrow.[4] To make matters worse, the State Department experts on Greece and Turkey, whatever their individual qualifications, were often as unknown to the secretary of state or the senior troubleshooter as the region itself. In a crisis, the secretary will understandably turn to people he knows, even if their knowledge of the problem is no more profound than his own. Aside from his immediate staff, those who are known to him are those working on the problems that get his attention. Greece, Turkey, and Cyprus, as we have seen, are rarely in that category. If the experts are strangers to him, the secretary may turn to people whom he knows in other agencies or outside government. He may rely very heavily on contacts of his own with the region and its personalities, however fleeting and subjective. In the summer of 1974, after the fall of the Greek military junta and the return of Constantine Karamanlis to head a provisional civilian government, Secretary of State Kissinger lost precious time because his single encounter with Karamanlis at a dinner party in Paris a year or two before had led him to believe that Karamanlis saw himself as a "Greek de Gaulle," who would steer Greece on a neutralist course and who took Soviet intentions lightly.

Furthermore, the Dulles, Ball, Acheson, Vance, and Sisco initiatives were undertaken with a minimum of preliminary groundwork in the three countries themselves, and at the breakneck speed that has come to characterize top-level U.S. diplomatic missions. Comprehensiveness is valued over depth and promptness over perspective. The final report of the Vance mission catches the flavor of urgency that pervaded the diplomacy of the Johnson administration (and is never absent from U.S. diplomatic conduct at the most senior levels): "At 11:30 on November 22 (1967)," the report reads, "Under Secretary [of State] Katzenbach, on authority of the President, telephoned former Deputy Secretary of Defense [Cyrus R.] Vance (to request him to undertake an emergency mission to Greece and Turkey) . . . [and] 20 minutes later, after consulting his [law] partners, he accepted. Three hours later Mr. Vance left for the airport on his way to Ankara."[5]

It says a great deal about Vance's dedication and diplomatic skills that he undertook his mission on such incredibly short notice and that he succeeded in averting a threatened Turkish landing in northern Cyprus of the kind that no one prevented seven years later. But it would be too much to expect that a diplomatic initiative launched on twenty minutes' notice, in which the principal negotiator was being provided key information aboard the aircraft carrying him into the center of the conflict, could do more than treat its symptoms.

It is true that long-term settlements can sometimes be negotiated under pressure of a crisis that would be impossible to achieve otherwise—the Lausanne Treaty of 1923, to which Greece and Turkey are signatories, is one example, since it followed the crushing defeat of a Greek expeditionary force by the Turkish army the year before. It is doubtful, however, that issues as complex as those that have led up to more recent crises— Cyprus, the Aegean shelf, territorial sea and air space, and the interpretation of treaties affecting the Aegean islands—combining as they do political, economic, and legal factors, bristling as they are with age-old animosities, could be settled in crisis conditions.

The terms of reference of the Vance mission, in any case, were confined to symptoms, not causes. In taking off from New York for Turkey Vance was told, "You are there [in Ankara] to offer your services, and those of the U.S. Government, to Turkey in a continuing effort to avert catastrophe."[6] The final report on his mission notes, "The Vance Mission properly eschewed responsibility for long-term solutions to this terrible problem [Cyprus]."

Vance's efforts "averted catastrophe" and bought time for Greece and Turkey, with whatever help the United States could supply, to address underlying problems. Unfortunately, as is often the case, the time was not constructively used. In 1967, Greece and Turkey were not ready, unaided, to negotiate compromises to problems that had so recently brought them to the brink of war. Senior levels of the U.S. government, so avid for details as a crisis develops, quickly lose interest when it subsides. The conduct of U.S. foreign policy, as the events of 1967 show with particular clarity, is geared to diplomatic firefighting, not fire prevention.

The November 1967 crisis was provoked by an attack against two Turkish Cypriot villages by the Cypriot national guard, composed of Greek Cypriots and led by mainland Greek officers. The attack was encouraged, if not planned, by the Greek military junta that had seized power in Athens the previous April. It resulted in the death of 28 Turkish Cypriots and immediate preparations by the Turkish government to intervene militarily. The crisis followed the rejection by Ankara in September of a long-term solution to the Cyprus problem, proposed by Athens, that would have involved unification of the island with Greece (*enosis*), in exchange for granting Turkey a military base there. This was a formula similar to one, the so-called Acheson Plan, proposed by the United States in 1964. On that occasion, it was rejected by Athens. In 1967, the United States did not involve itself in the Greek diplomatic initiative, probably because it was still trying to keep its distance from the Greek military government, against which Washington had levied an embargo on heavy-arms transfers immediately after the Athens coup.

This pattern of events is one we will observe repeatedly in the course of examining Greek-Turkish problems and the ways in which the United States has tried to deal with them. When tensions between Greece and Turkey are high, compromise is unthinkable; when low, unnecessary. When the United States is reminded by the high level of Greek-Turkish tension that a permanent settlement is needed, conditions are least suitable for one to be negotiated, and crisis diplomacy must settle for less.

Over time, settling for less can make "more" hard to achieve, because underlying problems are put to one side where they accumulate. None of the issues that led up to the 1967 crisis, or that aggravated it, has been resolved. All, in fact, are farther from solution than they were then—before the introduction of Turkish troops into northern Cyprus, the collapse of NATO's Aegean command-and-control arrangements, and the general hardening of positions that took place in 1974. These were catastrophes the Vance mission was not asked to avert because no one at the working level of the U.S. government was prepared to look that far ahead, and no one at the policy level knew enough about the underlying problems to *see* that far ahead.

Policy planning—the process of addressing problems that have not yet arisen—is not, of course, something that comes easily or naturally to any U.S. administration, whether in foreign or domestic policy. Our system functions in phases that are determined less by the complexity of the problems we face than by their political visibility and the time available to an administration to deal with them. In the case of Greece, Turkey, and Cyprus, unfamiliarity with the region at senior levels of the U.S. government usually combines at the working level with the bureaucratic preference we have already noted to treat each country separately in order, it is hoped, to limit the collateral damage that Greek-Turkish clashes, whether over Cyprus or something else, invariably inflict on the relations of both countries with the United States.

Bureaucratic and political priorities thus conspire to discourage the development of a long-term policy capable of promoting the settlement of problems as intractable as those of Greece and Turkey. U.S. policymakers are for the most part political appointees whose authority will expire with that of an administration. It is easier, and usually more politically rewarding, for them to cope with a crisis than with a condition. The former will quickly explode or be defused; the administration will be visibly engaged in important work to preserve or restore peace. The latter will be more ambiguous and protracted; much of the administration's work, if it is to be effective, will be invisible and—worse yet—is more likely to become visible if it fails than if it succeeds. At the working level of the administration, career officials suffer from fewer time constraints than their political superiors but approach problems on a narrower basis. Long-range planning requires breadth of vision, as well as depth of vision, and the instinct of working-level experts, unless there is insistent exhortation from above, is to keep problems small and manageable.[7]

As Henry Kissinger once observed, when events are compartmentalized by experts, insufficient attention is given to their overall effect, and the government spends more time "deciding where [it] is than where [it] is going."[8] One might add that when policies are formulated without reference to the experts, the government may go in circles, because it does not know where it is or where it has been before. A conspicuous weakness of U.S. policy toward Greece, Turkey, and Cyprus since 1947 has been that the experts seldom knew where they were going and the policymakers seldom knew where they were. No meeting on Cyprus in the White House situation room would be complete without someone asking, "Where is it on the map?" No trip back to the State Department would be complete without someone asking, "Where do they think they're headed?"

The United States is a continental power with global responsibilities, and Greece, Turkey, and Cyprus are not. It would be unrealistic to expect senior U.S. policymakers to be as conscious on a daily basis of the designs and sensibilities of these countries as their officials, whether they like it or not, must be of ours. In the U.S. foreign affairs apparatus, this is the job of career officials at the working level. A well-orchestrated foreign policy requires reliable, two-way communications between them and their policymaking superiors. When such communications do not exist—which, given the distrust of career officials ritually displayed by most presidential administrations, is often the case in the making of U.S. foreign policy—diplomatic initiatives fail, and serious misunderstandings are left in their wake.

Sometimes this is the result of the failure of working-level officials to alert the policymakers to impending danger. The coup of the Greek Colonels in April 1967 seems to have taken the U.S. government by surprise and, to some extent, we are still paying for our failure to develop a defensible policy toward the Greek military regime. The same could be said of our confused response to the anti-Greek riots in Istanbul in 1955, the scope and implications of which were inadequately appreciated or evaluated at the time.

Sometimes the misunderstandings are the result of the inclination of policymakers to treat Greece, Turkey, and Cyprus as components of a strategic equation rather than as states with long histories and military and diplomatic priorities based on regional concerns that may or may not be compatible with the global strategy of the United States. Approaching them in this way has induced a kind of tone deafness in U.S. policymaking and has led to serious miscalculations at critical moments.

When the Kennedy administration decided, in the context of the Cuban missile crisis of 1962, that Jupiter missiles had outlived their usefulness in Turkey and should be removed, the United States proceeded to do so with the same single-minded preoccupation with its military objectives that it had shown three years earlier when Washington convinced Ankara to accept the Jupiters over strenuous Soviet objections. When the Ford administration decided in the fall of 1974 that the Sixth Fleet's homeport program, which had been inadvisedly negotiated with the unpopular government of the Greek junta two years before, was creating more problems than it solved, it was so impatient to pull U.S. personnel out of Greece that it nearly failed to take into account the effect this move would have on the base negotiations the United States was about to begin with the new Greek government, which had been brought to power by a landslide vote in popular elections.

Although Turkey, Greece, and Cyprus all aligned themselves with the United States in the Persian Gulf crisis that began in August 1990, and military facilities on their territory were all used to support the campaign against Iraq, we have not always seen eye to eye on Middle Eastern questions, especially when Israel was involved, and our views will doubtless diverge again in the future. Before virtually unanimous agreement to oppose

Iraqi aggression against Kuwait was obtained in the United Nations, important restraints had been placed by Greece and Turkey on our ability to use indigenous military facilities in Middle Eastern contingencies. One reason was that U.S. troop movements and resupply operations through U.S. bases located or co-located on Greek and Turkish soil had taken place during the Middle Eastern crises of 1958, 1967, and 1973 (as well as on other, less dramatic occasions), about which the host countries believed they had been inadequately consulted.

Large powers like the United States need wide peripheral vision and skillful diplomacy if their influence is to achieve maximum effect at minimum cost. The replacement of British by U.S. influence in Greece and Turkey in 1947, and later in Cyprus, might have been expected to bring the replacement of British perceptions by American perceptions, and the formulation of policies better adapted to the changing situation in all three countries. Unfortunately, instead of formulating fresh Greek, Turkish, and Cypriot policies based on new assessments, Washington has tried, often clumsily, to fit Greece, Turkey, and Cyprus into its Soviet policy—to "contain" them in its policy of containment. As a consequence, after decades of the closest military collaboration with Greece and Turkey, our political relations with both remain uncertain and our economic relations undeveloped. In the case of Cyprus, our perspective has been similarly foreshortened, although the nonaligned status of the island and the existence there of military bases under British sovereignty have made the one-dimensional character of U.S. policy less apparent.

Military and economic assistance totaling over $13 billion to Turkey and $9 billion to Greece (between 1946 and 1987) has assured that what Greeks call "the American factor" has had significant influence on the policies of both states. It has not, however, created a sense of mutual trust, brought our respective priorities into closer alignment, or eased problems of communication. Too often, Greece and Turkey have entertained unrealistic expectations of the political or financial benefits that would accrue to them from their military relationships with the United States. Too often, U.S. influence has been wastefully expended

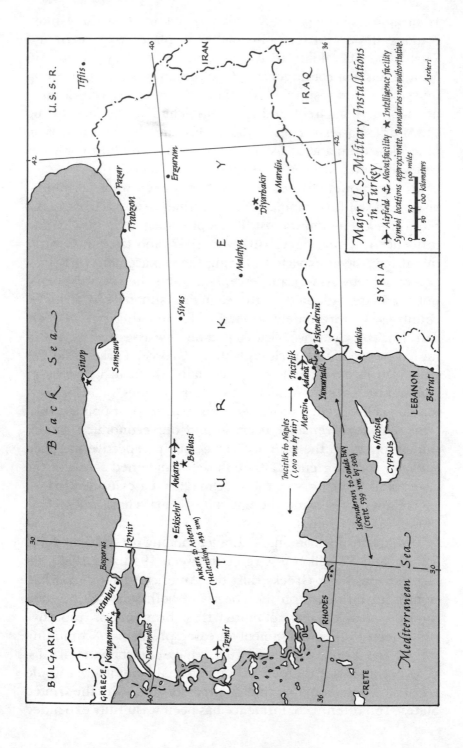

Major U.S. Military Installations in Turkey

✈ Airfield ⚓ Naval facility ★ Intelligence facility

Symbol locations approximate. Boundaries not authoritative.

0 50 100 miles
0 50 100 kilometers

Ascheri

to preserve or embellish prerogatives in our military relationships that needed to be trimmed down and adjusted to changing political and economic realities.

The U.S. ambassadors in Athens and Ankara, as well as their senior staffs, have spent inordinate amounts of time over the years seeking to avert or resolve problems arising from the relatively small U.S. military presence in both countries.[9] In periods when Ankara, Athens, and Washington agree on the nature of the actual or potential military threat they face, this presence is a welcome reassurance; at other times—more frequent and prolonged in recent years—it is a source of friction. In periods like these, disputes over legal jurisdiction in cases involving U.S. military personnel charged with off-duty misdemeanors, local tax liabilities, employment of U.S. dependents in on-base positions that could be filled by host country nationals, wage and hour disputes, even responsibility for trash collection, have become irritants entailing the kind of nit-picking negotiations one expects with adversaries rather than allies. On occasion, such problems have even had to be placed on the agendas of U.S. secretaries of state and defense for them to raise in their periodic meetings with Greek and Turkish ministers. The point is not that status-of-forces problems are unimportant. On the contrary, they are vexing and complicated in every country where U.S. troops are stationed. But the political cost of assuring satisfactory operating conditions at military facilities supposed to be serving common defense interests should not exceed their value, either to the United States or to the host country. When this happens, it usually means that more than the military relationship is out of kilter and that attention must be paid to the political and economic caulking that keeps the military relationship from leaking.

Although the Truman Doctrine and the North Atlantic Treaty were both cast in universal terms—the former declaring that "it must be the policy of the United States to support free peoples who are resisting attempted subjugation by armed minorities or by outside pressures," the latter that the signatories "are determined to safeguard the freedom, common heritage and civilization of their peoples, founded on the principles of

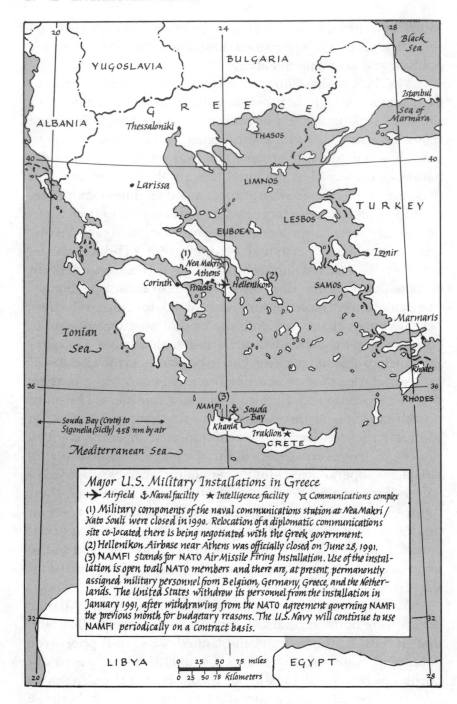

Major U.S. Military Installations in Greece

✈ Airfield ⚓ Naval facility ★ Intelligence facility ⌀ Communications complex

(1) Military components of the naval communications station at Nea Makri / Kato Souli were closed in 1990. Relocation of a diplomatic communications site co-located there is being negotiated with the Greek government.

(2) Hellenikon Airbase near Athens was officially closed on June 28, 1991.

(3) NAMFI stands for NATO Air Missile Firing Installation. Use of the installation is open to all NATO members and there are, at present, permanently assigned military personnel from Belgium, Germany, Greece, and the Netherlands. The United States withdrew its personnel from the installation in January 1991, after withdrawing from the NATO agreement governing NAMFI the previous month for budgetary reasons. The U.S. Navy will continue to use NAMFI periodically on a contract basis.

democracy, individual liberty and the rule of law"—the fact is that our relationship with Greece and Turkey was born of a particular circumstance—the perception that they were facing an imminent military threat from the Soviet bloc that was also a threat to us—at a particular time.

We shared, that is, a security threat more than we shared political values, economic interests, or a common historical experience. Indeed, since joining NATO, Greece and Turkey have both suspended free elections for periods of years without jeopardizing their alliance membership, and Turkey today has a parliamentary system of government that functions on the sufferance of the Turkish military, which has intervened to suspend it about once every decade since Turkey joined NATO. The form of government in Greece and Turkey has meant no more in terms of NATO privileges and immunities than it did when Portugal was invited to become a founding member for geostrategic reasons, although it had been governed by a fascist-style junta for 20 years and would continue to be so for another 22. Similarly, the commercial ties of the United States with Greece and Turkey, as well as with Cyprus, have been modest at best and, with the gradual reduction or elimination of U.S. economic aid and the rise of European trade, have dwindled further.[10] U.S. private investment unrelated to the offsets built into our military aid programs is minuscule in both countries. Finally, the U.S. relationship with Greece, Turkey, and Cyprus lacks historical resonance comparable to that felt by the Europeans, for whom Greek Hellenism and the Ottoman Turks represent, respectively, the origins and outer limits of their culture and heritage.

The "thinness" of the U.S. relationship with Greece, Turkey, and Cyprus might not be important if we could accept it for what it is. (As a British newspaper editor once said of a U.S. ambassador-designate, a political appointee who could not recall the name of the prime minister of the country to which he was being assigned, "At least he will not arrive at his new post with crippling preconceptions.") Moreover, the strategic prominence of Turkey in the eyes of U.S. policymakers and the political prominence of over a million well-organized Greek-Americans in the eyes of Congress, add real substance to our relations with Athens and

Ankara although, as we shall see, they also add tensions and complications.

What often confuses our relations more than their lopsided reliance on military considerations are the expedients to which Washington resorts in attempting to conceal this reality. In the case of Turkey, this means finding in our security relationship moral and ethical properties that would be extraneous to it even if they were not largely imaginary. The preamble to the 1980 Defense and Economic Cooperation Agreement (DECA) claimed, for example, that the U.S.-Turkish relationship rested on "the principles of democracy, human rights, justice and social progress" and, even as the U.S. government pledged to use its "best efforts" to obtain higher military aid for Turkey, expressed faith "in the acceleration of disarmament efforts."[11] These claims seem excessive and misleading even when allowance is made for the often sanctimonious language of diplomacy. A more insidious effect is that, over time, the parties to agreements cloaked in this kind of moralistic language come to believe the claims made by it and become disillusioned when they are proved hollow. In 1980, the United States and Turkey would probably have put their security relationship on firmer ground by describing it with greater precision and candor while making fewer hyperbolic claims about what it represented in moral terms.

In the case of Greece, there has been less need to simulate common democratic values (at least since the fall of the Greek military junta in 1974) but more need to simulate common military purposes. This was especially true between 1981 and 1989, when the Papandreou government, although it did not carry out its campaign pledge to withdraw Greece from NATO, sought in every possible way to differentiate its foreign and security policies from those of the alliance. Thus, the U.S.-Greek DECA negotiated with the Papandreou government in 1983 was refreshingly free of preambular bombast but not of calculated ambiguity designed to conceal the fact that joint military facilities, whose existence was extended by the agreement, would support NATO missions.[12] Remarkably, in an agreement between two members of the same military alliance, no specific reference to NATO was made anywhere in the text. Article I stated only that defense cooperation between the United States and Greece was based on "existing . . . multilateral agreements."[13] The 1980 U.S.-Turkish DECA, on the other hand, referred four times to NATO in the preamble alone. This was because the Turks wished to emphasize what the Greeks wished to camouflage, namely, that U.S. facilities on the soil of both countries served NATO purposes. It is an odd consequence of the Papandreou government's attitude that nowhere in the 1983 U.S.-Greek DECA was there a clear statement of the external purposes to be served by military cooperation between the parties or by U.S. facilities in Greece. In the edgy state of U.S.-Greek relations in 1983, the only way to simulate a common military purpose was to refrain from referring to any purpose at all.

We have, therefore, essentially military relationships with Greece and Turkey, the purposes of which we define, depending on political expediency, as either more or less than they are. There is no reason why a military relationship cannot endure as long as or longer than any other if the security threat that brought it into being persists and the relationship itself is intelligently managed—managed, that is, with constant attention to its nonmilitary aspects. This is what the United States has often failed to do in the case of Greece and Turkey and has also discouraged NATO from doing. Instead of using wide peripheral vision and skillful diplomacy, we have too often been inattentive to nonmilitary aspects of our relationship and, when they could no longer be ignored, have tried to make them go away by a kind of diplomacy by incantation.

We can gain a better understanding of the shortcomings of this approach by examining two diplomatic breakdowns from the early years of our special relationship with Greece and Turkey that were aggravated, if not caused, by Washington's lack of peripheral vision. The first developed out of the reaction of the U.S. government to Greek-Turkish differences over Cyprus in 1955, only three years after the two countries were admitted to NATO and at a time when Cyprus was still a British Crown colony. The similarly worded letters that Secretary of State Dulles conveyed that September to the prime ministers of Greece and Turkey expressed an official attitude toward their differences that not only declined to take sides but seemed to deny that there were sides to take. Greece, whose minority in Istanbul had just been victimized by violent demonstrations, reacted with exasperation and, not for the last time, protested by withdrawing its forces from NATO exercises in which the Turks were also scheduled to participate.

Nine years later, in 1964, the United States was still having trouble seeing what all the fuss was about between the Greeks and the Turks. This time it was the Turkish minority in Cyprus that had been victimized, and Ankara seemed to be on the verge of military intervention. The letter addressed that June by President Johnson to the Turkish prime minister was so harshly worded that the Turks reacted, also not for the last time, by placing stringent new controls on U.S. military facilities in Turkey.

In these two cases our unswerving pursuit of U.S. strategic objectives led us to brush aside everything that seemed incompatible with them and, in the end, inflicted lasting damage not only on U.S. relations with Greece and Turkey but on the security posture our actions were supposed to protect. The Dulles and Johnson letters deserve a closer look, both for what they reveal about U.S. policy toward Greece and Turkey in the past and what they suggest for it in the future.

2

THE DULLES AND JOHNSON LETTERS: TOO MUCH, TOO LATE

The responsibility that the United States inherited from Britain in 1947 for the defense of Greece and Turkey, first under the Truman Doctrine and from 1952 in the context of NATO, had no direct effect on the status of Cyprus, which had become a British Crown colony in 1925. In the events leading up to Cypriot independence in 1960, therefore, the United States was an interested observer but not a participant. The habit that we acquired early of regarding Cyprus essentially in terms of its relations with Greece and Turkey has persisted to the present day. As one expert put it, "Americans . . . have tended to think of Cyprus as a problem, more than as a country with which to conduct normal state to state business."[1]

When, in 1955, Greek Cypriot sentiment in favor of uniting the island with Greece began to meet unyielding British resistance, the demand for *enosis*—union—turned from a political slogan into a battle cry. A clandestine guerrilla organization, EOKA (whose Greek initials stood for the National Organization of Cypriot Fighters) was created under the command of Lt. Col. George Grivas, a Cypriot-born officer of the Greek army with a history of right-wing political extremism. Starting in the spring of 1955, EOKA, operating from secret bases in the rugged Troodos Mountains of central Cyprus, launched a campaign of terrorism and sabotage against British rule. Although British military and colonial authorities were the prime target of Grivas and his guerrillas, EOKA terrorists claimed many victims among Greek Cypriots reputed to be collaborators of the British, as well as some Turkish Cypriots and at least one American, a member of the consular staff killed in 1956 in the bombing of a bar frequented by British troops.

Washington's policy at this time, in the first term of the Eisenhower administration, with Soviet machinations perceived everywhere, was to support the British, deplore terrorism, and keep an anxious eye on the effects of violence in Cyprus on the security of NATO's southeastern flank. The Cyprus problem was a distraction from the overriding need to contain Soviet expansion, and any outcome of the struggle for *enosis* was likely to be less desirable than the existing status of the island: Victory for EOKA would alienate the Turks; defeat would alienate the Greeks; and if neither side prevailed, in a climate of escalating violence, British relations with Greece would be irreparably damaged. Even the prospect of inscribing Cyprus on the agenda of the UN General Assembly filled Washington with apprehension, since it would permit the Soviets to assume an anticolonialist stance, which the United States, in this instance, was reluctant to adopt. Since Turkey supported the continuation of British colonial rule, British Cyprus presented fewer strategic uncertainties for NATO than a Greek or independent Cyprus. The trouble was political, since then, as now, there seemed to be little margin for compromise among the interested parties. It was, however, a British colonial problem and the United States was satisfied to leave it that way. As long as Britain was intent on maintaining its position in the Middle East and in keeping open the Suez Canal as a primary line of communication to the Indian Ocean, military considerations were paramount. Cyprus was seen in London as an essential forward base. Anthony Eden was reflecting this outlook in 1954 when he replied "never" when the Greek prime minister, Alexander Papagos, asked him at what point the British government would consider granting *enosis*. This was probably the moment at which the Greek government and the Greek Cypriots decided that diplomacy alone would not change the status of Cyprus. Grivas arrived secretly in Cyprus within months of the Papagos-Eden exchange and began to recruit and train EOKA guerrillas.

Greece's tougher attitude toward the British was made possible by another factor. As long as Greece depended primarily on Britain to resist the military challenge of Greek communism, restraint in seeking *enosis* was unavoidable. As British influence in Greece was replaced by American after 1947, the Greeks felt freer to oppose British policy in Cyprus openly and to work actively for unification. As the level of violence on the island mounted after 1955, Washington found itself caught uncomfortably between Athens and London and had more reason to urge the British to seek diplomatic remedies to the Cyprus problem. For Britain, the turning point came with the Suez campaign of 1956 when, under pressure from the United States, British, French, and Israeli forces abandoned their invasion of Egypt without achieving either of their principal objectives—to remove the Nasser government and to restore international control of the Suez Canal. Although the Suez campaign confirmed the military value of Cyprus for airborne operations in the middle East, it also conclusively demonstrated that, even with Cyprus as a base, Britain was too weak to keep the canal open and maintain its Middle Eastern position. The strategic rationale for keeping Cyprus British had ceased to be decisive, and the alternatives of *enosis* or independence seemed suddenly within reach. Cyprus could no longer be treated as though it were exclusively a British colonial problem.

Thus, the United States, while playing a passive role in developments that led up to the independence of Cyprus in 1960, nevertheless exercised an important indirect influence on Greek and British policy after 1947 and bore a significant responsibility for the outcome. The Truman Doctrine had freed the Greeks from their dependence on the British and enabled them to join with the Greek Cypriots in using violent means to overthrow British rule; and Washington's frustration of the Suez operation had revealed to the Greeks, the Turks, and the Cypriots the extent to which British power had weakened in the eastern Mediterranean, including, in all probability, its grip on Cyprus. It was the first of many periods in our relations with Cyprus, Greece, and Turkey when we underestimated the extent to which regional concerns would influence their behavior and overshadowed the global missions we had assigned to them. As tension in Cyprus built up in 1955, instead of relying almost entirely on military blueprints and what we construed to be the requirements of global security to determine U.S. policy, we might have been able to play a more constructive role had we remembered that most diplomacy, like all politics, is local.[2]

In the summer of 1955, more than a year before the Suez crisis, Britain sought to avert a full-scale insurgency in Cyprus by means of concessions that it hoped would appease the Greeks and Greek Cypriots without causing an explosion in Turkey. A conference was organized in London to which the Greeks and Turks were invited, although Athens protested against the inclusion of Turkey, and Ankara feared that some form of *enosis* would be proposed by Britain and Greece. The conference opened on August 29 with the Greeks threatening to withdraw because of the Turkish presence and the Turks looking for ways to demonstrate that the concerns of the Turkish Cypriot minority—consisting of 18 percent of the island's population—and the island's location only 40 miles off the Anatolian coast gave Ankara a legitimate stake in the future of Cyprus. In the course of a week of meetings little progress was made. The Greeks were confirmed in their belief that Turkey would prevent meaningful talks, the Turks in their suspicion that Britain and Greece were moving toward a solution involving self-determination for Cyprus and a settlement that took insufficient account of Turkish interests.

On September 6, 1955, the day before the London Conference was scheduled to end, a bomb exploded in the courtyard of the Turkish consulate in Thessaloniki, which was adjacent to the house where the founder of modern Turkey, Kemal Ataturk, had been born when that northern Greek port was still a part of the Ottoman Empire. Subsequently, Turkish court testimony presented at the treason trials of leading members of the Menderes government in 1960 suggested that the bomb had been planted by Turkish agents, but, at the time, the episode was considered by a large majority of Turks to be an outrageous Greek provocation, and the repercussions in Turkey were almost immediate. Ostensibly spontaneous demonstrations in Istanbul and Izmir, protesting the Thessaloniki bombing and supporting Turkish Cypriot rights, turned into anti-Greek riots and resulted in the pillaging of Greek property and the terrorization of the still sizable Greek minority, many of whom now left Turkey never to return. These events also produced new tensions in Cyprus where the intimidation of the Turkish minority by pro-*enosis* extremists was already a problem.

It was at this point that the United States, which had been monitoring the London Conference but expressing no views of its own, decided that, as leader of the Western Alliance—which Greece and Turkey had joined only three years before—it could no longer avoid taking a position. The position taken by the Eisenhower administration ignored the issues in dispute between Greece and Turkey and downplayed the significance of injury done to the Istanbul Greeks. It was an unsatisfactory compromise developed by the Office of Greek, Turkish, and Iranian Affairs on the basis of insufficient intelligence as to the cause of the Istanbul riots, inadequate consultation with the U.S. embassies in Athens and Ankara as to the attitudes of the Greek and Turkish governments, and under the usual pressure from policymaking levels to show that the administration was not "standing idly by."[3]

Secretary of State Dulles was advised by NEA and GTI to address identical letters to the prime ministers of Greece and Turkey reminding them that it was their duty to subordinate their bilateral differences to the larger interests of the NATO alliance and to their special relationship with the United States. No reference was made in the text of the letters to the Istanbul riots, because the Turkish desk did not wish the secretary of state to appear to be holding the Turkish government responsible for events that Ankara had publicly deplored, and no one in Washington was yet aware that the riots were other than spontaneous reactions to the bombing of Ataturk's birthplace. The Greek desk, on the other hand, was acutely aware that twelve days had gone by with no official expression of sympathy for the Greek victims by the U.S. government. It was therefore decided that even though Dulles would not refer to the riots in his letters to the two prime ministers, an accompanying statement would be released to the press expressing the regrets of the United States over the events in Istanbul and Izmir. Public release of the text of the letters, which was virtually simultaneous with their delivery in Athens and Ankara, was intended to intensify pressure on the two governments to compose their differences while emphasizing the impartiality of the United States.

On September 18, the State Department issued a press release, noting that the United States "regards as most regrettable recent evidences of tension between the governments of Greece and Turkey" that "resulted last week in widespread violence in the cities of Istanbul and Izmir," leading the United States to express to the Turkish government its "deep concern."[4] Although the Greek desk considered the department's cautiously worded condolence something of a victory over the Turkish desk's objections to any statement imputing responsibility to Turkish authorities, public opinion in Greece, which had been calling with ever-increasing stridency for the United States to condemn Turkish actions, was unaware of the small bureaucratic triumph. The world press devoted headline attention to the evenhanded letters from Dulles to prime ministers Adnan Menderes and Alexander Papagos but scarcely mentioned U.S. "regrets" or "concern" over the events that prompted them.

The letters themselves, however, raised a storm of protest in Greece where they were seen as putting the victim on the same level as the assailant. The Greek ambassador in Washington was quoted in the *New York Times* on September 19 as having said, "This is very disappointing. It doesn't give the slightest touch of moral comfort to the Greeks who suffered this unimaginable attack at the hands of so-called friends and allies. It is sad that this is the outcome of ten days' thinking at the department."[5] The opposition Liberal Democratic party of former (and future) prime minister George Papandreou was less restrained: "We doubt," said a party spokesman, "whether such a document, addressed to a free and independent country from her allies, had its like in the world's diplomatic history."[6] Prime Minister Papagos responded to Dulles on September 21 in tones of suppressed emotion worthy of the State Department itself:

> I am obliged . . . to observe that as a whole your message . . . does not correspond to the true development of events. . . . The Turkish people's hostility to Greece . . . was manifested by unheard-of violence in Istanbul and Izmir, on the occasion of a friendly conference of the three countries which took place behind closed doors in London, without even the slightest provocation on our part. Fol-

lowing the indescribably tragic events in Turkey, of which I am certain you must have been fully informed, we reasonably expect the moral and material reparation due to us from the Turkish Government. . . . [7]

Turkish reaction to the parallel letters reflected obvious gratification that Ankara was being called to show more statesmanship than remorse. Prime Minister Menderes set the tone in his reply to Dulles:

> I find great satisfaction in immediately and warmly thanking you for your expressed conviction that the Turkish-Greek friendship and alliance forms a solid bulwark in the eastern Mediterranean and that this friendship and alliance will not be disrupted by the recent events and for your sincere hope that there will be a renewal of Turkish-Greek cooperation despite the recent deplorable incidents. . . . I want to stress the point that the atmosphere of nervous tension steadily aggravated by the Cyprus question during the past year culminated in the September 7 incidents—which we shall always remember with grief and regret—which were organized by the clandestine Communist organization and leftist elements [seizing] an opportunity that will never again be present. . . . [8]

Less gratifying to the Eisenhower administration as time went by were the views of U.S. commentators, most of whom noted the contrast between the Greek and Turkish reactions and concluded that, whatever the State Department's intention, the parallel letters had put the United States on a collision course with Greece. C. L. Sulzberger, writing in the *New York Times* on September 24, observed, "Whoever advised the Secretary on phrasing his message pulled a prize boner. The Greeks are now even angrier than they were. Mr. Dulles' words had the effect of gasoline poured on fire. And although our Athens embassy cautiously proposed we had better back Greece's viewpoint in the agenda argument on Cyprus at the United Nations General Assembly, we did the opposite. This has not helped our moral prestige." [9]

The text of the Dulles letters[10] that so outraged the Greeks and gratified the Turks contains diplomatic pieties that have been reformulated on countless subsequent occasions by American policymakers exhorting Athens and Ankara to place the interests of NATO (and the United States) above their own. Sometimes the Greeks have been offended, sometimes the

Turks, but these schoolmasterly calls to order have brought the two allies no closer to NATO than to each other.

"I have followed with concern," said Dulles, "the dangerous deterioration of Greek-Turkish relations caused by the Cyprus question. Regardless of the causes of this disagreement, which are complex and numerous, I believe that the unity of the North Atlantic community, which is the basis of our common security, must be restored without delay." After invoking the spirit of allied partnership in NATO and on the Korean battlefield, the secretary continued, "I cannot believe that in the face of this record of common achievement, any problem will long disrupt the course of Turkish-Greek friendship. Nor can I believe that the unhappy events of the past two weeks will reverse policies of cooperation which were initiated twenty-five years ago under the far-sighted leadership of Kemal Ataturk and Eleftherios Venizelos."

A 500-year antagonism, already historic when Columbus discovered America, was thus deemed less significant than the period of détente that began in 1930 and lasted for ten years[11]; and the Cyprus dispute, which had just caused riots that were later described as "the beginning of the end for the historic Greek community in Turkey"[12] was brushed off as a problem with "complex and numerous" causes but no apparent claim on the attention of the United States or NATO.

The Dulles letters then went on to explain why the United States felt justified in calling its two allies to order:

> Since 1947, the United States has made very considerable efforts to assist Greece and Turkey to maintain their freedom and to achieve greater social and economic progress. We have extended this assistance—and extend it now—because we believe that the partnership of Greece and Turkey constitutes a strong bulwark of the free world in a critical area.
>
> If that bulwark should be materially weakened, the consequences could be grave indeed. I urge you therefore to make every effort to assure that the effectiveness of your partnership is not impaired by present disagreements.

The minatory undertone of these paragraphs was not lost on the Greeks, who felt doubly aggrieved by the implication that U.S. aid might be jeopardized if they did not tone down their protests to the Turks. They viewed the letter as "blackmail," according to the conservative Athenian newspaper, *Ethnos*.

The Dulles letters merit no more than a footnote in the diplomatic history of U.S. relations with Greece and Turkey. The episode is instructive, however, because it illustrates how the "small picture" focus of working-level experts and the "big picture" perspective of policymakers can produce fuzzy policies that lead to clear misunderstandings, especially when compounded by Washington's failure to consult U.S. embassies in the capitals directly affected by U.S. pronouncements. The State Department's Greek and Turkish desks, engaged in their debate over how far it was permissible for the United States to go in publicly imputing responsibility to the Turkish government for the Istanbul riots, were concerned about preserving appearances in our bilateral relations. What could the United States say to mollify the Greeks that would not outrage the Turks? Dulles and his senior advisors, including the regional assistant secretary, were concerned about preserving the appearance of NATO solidarity on the southeastern flank. What could the United States say that would cause Greece and Turkey to back off without affording the Soviets a tactical opening? The Dulles letters were fashioned to fit the smaller bureaucratic and larger geopolitical needs of the U.S. government, not the diplomatic requirements of the specific problem at hand.

Our inattention to diplomatic realities in 1955 had costs of a kind that would recur in our ongoing security relationship with Greece and Turkey. The Greek government reacted to the Istanbul riots—and the apparently complaisant attitudes of the United States and NATO—by withdrawing its forces from announced NATO maneuvers in the Mediterranean.[13] The Menderes government, which had declared martial law in Ankara, Istanbul, and Izmir following the riots, as well as suspending publication of four newspapers that had given undue prominence to the Dulles letters, deplored Greece's withdrawal, which the Turkish prime minister accurately but disingenuously termed "a disquieting precedent for the future of NATO." The Soviet Union in the person of the Orthodox Patriarch of Moscow sent a message of condolence to the Ecumenical Patriarch in Istanbul, expressing his "deepest love toward the church of

Constantinople" and his hope that God "will extend his Almighty Hand to chastise and paralyze those who unleashed violence."[14] Meanwhile, the most effective diplomacy on behalf of the United States was conducted, as has not infrequently been the case in Greek-Turkish confrontations, by a military man, Adm. William M. Fechtler, commander-in-chief of Allied Forces, Southern Europe (CINCSOUTH), who promptly paid quick visits to Greece and Turkey. Less inhibited than the State Department's regional desk chiefs by bureaucratic considerations, he referred in Athens to the Istanbul riots by saying, "I thoroughly understand the Greek viewpoint. We want to cure this situation."[15] His was the only expression of sympathy by a senior U.S. official that was reported in the Greek press.

Almost a decade passed between the Dulles and Johnson letters. Difficult, three-cornered negotiations among the British, Greeks, and Turks resulted in independence for the Republic of Cyprus in 1960 under a constitution providing for a Greek Cypriot president, a Turkish Cypriot vice president, and an intricate system of checks and balances designed to protect the rights of the Turkish Cypriot minority without paralyzing the republic's ability to function as a sovereign state which had become a member of the United Nations in the year of its independence. Lacking the trust needed to make so complex a system work, troubles began almost immediately between the Greek and Turkish Cypriot communities.

By late 1963, the president of Cyprus, the Greek Orthodox archbishop Makarios, had become convinced that the 1960 constitution was unworkable, and in November he submitted to his Turkish Cypriot vice president, Fazil Kutchuk, thirteen proposed amendments that would have had the effect of drastically reducing the powers and representation guaranteed to the Turkish Cypriots. When these proposals were rejected by Kutchuk, with the backing of the Turkish government, a full-blown crisis ensued and intercommunal violence broke out on the island. The Turkish Cypriots, numbering only 110,000 of the island's population of more than 600,000, were heavily outnumbered and suffered severe casualties in the fighting. On Christmas Day 1963 the Turkish air force flew low-level sorties over the Cypriot capital of Nicosia and the 650-man Turkish garrison—which was authorized by the 1960 independence treaties, along with a Greek garrison of 950 men—took up positions along the road from Nicosia to the port of Kyrenia on the north coast. Turkish military intervention seemed imminent.

As it had earlier, in the period that culminated in the Dulles letters of September 1955, the United States tried—with better and more understandable reason during this period of resurgent Greek Turkish tension—to leave the handling of the crisis to Britain, a guarantor of the 1960 Zurich and London agreements and a principal drafter of the Cypriot constitution. President John F. Kennedy had been assassinated in November 1963, only a week before Archbishop Makarios had submitted his ill-fated proposals to amend the constitution; South Vietnamese president Ngo Dinh Diem had been assassinated earlier in the month; a serious crisis was playing itself out in the Republic of the Congo (now Zaire), where a U.S.–Belgian military operation had been launched to rescue consular officials and missionaries held hostage by Congolese rebels; and President Johnson was just beginning to orient himself on the world stage, where he had so unexpectedly become a major player.

U.S. efforts not to be drawn into the Cyprus crisis of 1963–1964 were no more successful than they had been earlier. When a new London conference with Greeks, Turks, and Cypriots failed to resolve the deadlock in January, the British turned to the United States for help. This led early in 1964 to shuttle diplomacy by Under Secretary of State Ball; an abortive attempt to form a peacekeeping force of NATO members in February; the creation in March of the UN peacekeeping force (UNFICYP) that remains in Cyprus to this day; and finally—and, as we shall see, inconsistently—to the Johnson-Inönü letter of June 5, 1964.[16]

It is a reflection of the ephemeral nature of shuttle diplomacy, and the perverse ends it can serve when conducted by senior officials with little direct experience of the countries involved and without the benefit of carefully considered long-term polices, that Ball's mission, which his memoirs show to have inculcated in him an intense distrust and antipathy for the Greek and Greek Cypriot leadership, nevertheless terminated in President Johnson's brutally worded démarche to the Turkish prime minister, whom Ball admired.[17] It also resulted in notably unsuccessful visits to Washington by the Turkish and Greek prime ministers later that same month, during which both statesmen were urged to accept a Cyprus settlement based on double *enosis,* a proposal that many Greeks recall today with as much distaste as Turks do the Johnson letter.

The U.S. government, as we have seen, had up to that point played no real role in influencing political developments in Cyprus; had only a superficial appreciation of the larger Cyprus problem; and had involved itself reluctantly, at the last minute, at the request of the British and out of fear that the Soviets would otherwise find a way to intervene. Ball quotes with approval in his memoirs the judgement of two American journalists who subsequently asserted that his efforts had "prevented the establishment of a Soviet satellite in the eastern Mediterranean."[18] It is permissible in retrospect to doubt that Moscow planned, or even conceived as possible, the transformation of Cyprus into a Soviet satellite—an idea planted in Ball's head, incidentally, by Greek prime minister George Papandreou, who hoped to make President Johnson's flesh creep and gain U.S. support for *enosis.*[19] Moscow's Cyprus policy was mainly characterized by caution. While the Soviets called for the withdrawal of foreign troops (including British) from Cyprus, they avoided initiatives likely to provoke their Turkish neighbors and to lead to the partition of Cyprus by two NATO states. It should also have been clear, even in 1964, that Archbishop Makarios was by this time pursuing his own course—nonaligned, as it turned out, with Greece as well as with the superpowers. But a policy created on the run has no time for nuances. Ball himself probably said it best: "The moral is clear: effective diplomacy for a great nation requires constant high-quality institutional vigilance. That is not possible when all decisions are preempted by an individual virtuoso with a lust for travel."[20] (He was, of course, referring to a different Cypriot crisis—that of the summer of 1974—and a different virtuoso— Henry A. Kissinger.)

The Johnson letter itself is a startling specimen of diplomatic overkill. The text suggests that it was hastily drafted—

President Johnson writes to Prime Minister Inönü in the first paragraph that [U.S. ambassador to Turkey, Raymond Hare] "has indicated that you postponed your decision [to land Turkish troops in Cyprus] for a few hours in order to obtain my views." So does its excessive length—almost 2,000 words—since more time would have produced a less prolix and repetitious document. But even allowing for the administration's desire to act swiftly to forestall the threatened Turkish intervention, the president's language seems unnecessarily harsh. After the passage quoted above, he goes on to remonstrate, "I put to you personally whether you really believe that it is appropriate for your government, in effect, to present an ultimatum to an ally who has demonstrated such staunch support over the years as has the United States for Turkey."

The letter dismisses Turkish claims that intervention is permissible under the 1960 Treaty of Guarantee and then, in a passage that particularly outraged the Turks, raises in solemn terms the question of whether Ankara's proposed action would jeopardize its claim to the assistance of fellow members of NATO in the event of a Soviet attack on Turkey. The second paragraph of the letter reads:

> I must call to your attention also, Mr. Prime Minister, the obligations of NATO. There can be no question in your mind that a Turkish intervention in Cyprus would lead to a military engagement between Turkish and Greek forces. . . . Adhesion to NATO, in its very essence, means that NATO countries will not wage war on each other. Germany and France have buried centuries of animosity and hostility in becoming NATO allies; nothing less can be expected from Greece and Turkey. Furthermore, a military intervention in Cyprus by Turkey could lead to direct involvement by the Soviet Union. I hope you will understand that your NATO allies have not had the chance to consider whether they have an obligation to protect Turkey against the Soviet Union if Turkey takes a step which results in Soviet intervention without the full consent and understanding of its NATO allies."[21]

This is strong language, stronger by far than that of the Dulles letters. Ball terms it "the most brutal diplomatic note" he had ever seen.[22] Nevertheless, there are similarities between the Johnson and Dulles letters. Aside from its sententious tone—"nothing less can be expected from Greece and Turkey"—the Johnson message recalls Dulles's in another way. Dulles warned by implication that if Greece and Turkey did not bury their differences they might no longer be able to rely on the assistance of the United States and NATO to defend them from the Soviet threat; Johnson explicitly questions the validity of NATO guarantees if Turkish actions in Cyprus were to lead to Soviet involvement. Neither approach, it is safe to say, can have strengthened Turkish and Greek confidence in NATO, and one is left to wonder whether earlier and more perceptive attention by the United States and NATO to Greek-Turkish differences—the kind of "constant high-quality institutional vigilance" advocated by Ball—could have produced better results at less cost.

Before concluding this examination of the Johnson letter, we should note one curious feature that does not resemble anything in the Dulles text but does sound a plaintive chord that echoes throughout the history of U.S. diplomatic relations with both Greece and Turkey. The president, anticipating the effect of his words on the Turkish government, states to Inönü, "It is possible that you feel in Ankara that the United States has not been sufficiently active in your behalf." Then, to show how unjustified this feeling would be, he continues, "But surely you know that our policy has caused the liveliest resentment in Athens (where demonstrations have been aimed against us) and has led to a basic alienation between the United States and Archbishop Makarios." In short, U.S. policy deserved respect because it had outraged equally *all* the parties to the dispute.

The Turks, needless to say, did not look at it that way. They called off their plans for military intervention in Cyprus, but Turkish-U.S. relations were rocked by the Johnson letter, which caused Ankara to reassess its dependence on NATO and to rethink Turkish relations with the Soviet Union. In 1965, the Turks requested that the United States stop using Turkish bases for reconnaissance flights over Soviet territory and began a deliberate, if gradual, process of political and economic accommodation with Moscow which, among other things, made Turkey in the 1970s one of the largest recipients of Soviet economic assistance outside the Warsaw Pact.[23]

Even after allowing for the improvised character of much that passes for policymaking in the U.S. government, the origins of the Johnson letter remain somewhat puzzling. Although its Olympian tone suggests White House authorship, we are told by George Ball that the letter was drafted by Secretary of State Dean Rusk, together with senior State Department aides, who showed it to him on June 4, 1964, before Rusk had finished working on it. Ball says that he commented, "I think that may stop Inönü from invading, but I don't know how we'll ever get him down off the ceiling after that."[24] He does not indicate that he attempted to dissuade the secretary of state from sending such a peremptory draft to the president or that he recommended any change in the tone, although he makes clear elsewhere that he believes the Cypiot crisis of 1963–1964 to have been provoked by Archbishop Makarios, repeatedly expresses his disdain for Prime Minister Papandreou, and praises the leadership qualities of Prime Minister Inönü.

The explanation for the jarring inconsistency between the Johnson letter as drafted by Rusk and the evaluation of the Greek-Turkish-Cypriot situation by Ball, his principal deputy, probably lies in the highly personalized, strongly political style of presidential leadership in the Johnson administration. Ball makes it clear that the president followed the Cyprus crisis closely[25] and also that Johnson was concerned about its effects on American voters of Greek origin in the November elections later that year. It seems likely that Rusk, good soldier that he was, drafted the kind of letter to Inönü that he had reason to believe Johnson wanted to send.

Whatever the truth may be, we are left again with the impression that earlier, more attentive, and better-informed diplomacy on the part of the United States might have allowed less wounding words to be used later. In its dealings with Greece, Turkey, and Cyprus the United States seems continually to be playing catchup, reacting too late to threats to the peace in Cyprus and the Aegean and therefore reacting inappropriately, weighing regional problems on the scales of superpower military parity and therefore often weighing them incorrectly. The unsettling effect of this approach on our relations with all three is nowhere more apparent than in our military assistance policies toward Greece and Turkey.

3

THE 70 PERCENT SOLUTION TO OUR MILITARY AID DILEMMA

The apportionment of U.S. military assistance to Turkey and Greece has become an apple of discord almost as bitterly disputed by the recipients as the one Aphrodite received from Paris, which touched off the Trojan Wars.[1] Over the course of more than 40 years, from 1947 through 1991, U.S. military aid to Turkey has totaled over $9 billion and to Greece over $5 billion. The annual military aid proposals by the executive branch and the hearings that accompany the congressional authorization and appropriation process have become almost as familiar to the Greek and Turkish governments as they are to the Defense and State Departments. This has been especially true since the Cyprus crisis of 1974, when Turkish military occupation of about 36 percent of the island, following an Athens-engineered coup against the legal government of Cyprus, caused Congress, in February 1975, to impose an embargo on arms shipments to Turkey that was not lifted until August 1978.

It was at this time, in a 1978 amendment to the Foreign Assistance Act of 1961, that Congress, in lifting the embargo, specified that U.S. aid to Greece and Turkey should "be designed to insure that the present balance of military strength among countries of the region . . . is preserved."[2] If the term "present balance" had been left undefined, so general a condition would have been a weak constraint on the Greek and Turkish aid programs of any administration. For the Ford, Carter, Reagan, and Bush administrations—motivated by a desire to strengthen the largest standing army in NATO[3] after the American and compensate Turkey for the indignities and material losses suffered during the arms embargo—modernization of the Turkish armed forces has been a prime objective. The Aegean balance of power, as important as it is to Greece, has been a distinctly secondary consideration: Turkey, with its massive military force,

40

its strong military culture, and the desire of the Turkish leadership elite to associate the country more closely with Europe and the United States, had the reputation in Washington and NATO of being alliance-minded. Greece, on the other hand, was considered difficult, shrill in articulating its complaints against Turkey in NATO councils, often disposed to introduce bilateral problems into the military business of the alliance, tiresomely aggrieved and grieving. Left to their own devices in setting military aid levels, Washington policymakers would have worried less about the requirement for "Aegean balance" than the problem of extracting from Congress the colossal amounts they considered necessary to turn Turkey's large but decrepit military machine into a modern fighting force.[4]

Their margin for maneuver was sharply reduced, however, by the fact that when Congress lifted the Turkish arms embargo, it had already agreed on a definition of "Aegean balance." Accepting the views of the Greek government, a congressional majority, spearheaded by an articulate coalition of philhellenes, liberals, and conservatives with significant Greek-American constituencies, decided that the Aegean status quo would not be threatened if U.S. military assistance to Greece and Turkey were appropriated in a seven-to-ten ratio. Greece, that is, would be assured of receiving 70 percent of whatever amount was approved for Turkey.

How had the Greek government arrived at this figure? The best explanation that the author has heard comes from a senior Greek diplomat who was involved in the 7:10 calculation in 1976, at a time when Greece and the United States were negotiating a new Defense and Economic Cooperation Agreement. Parallel negotiations between Turkey and the United States had been concluded in Ankara in March 1976 with the signing of an agreement that included a U.S. commitment to seek $1 billion in military aid for Turkey over the four-year duration of the DECA. This amount was far in excess of aid levels that the U.S. delegation had been discussing with the Greeks. With their customary penchant for compartmentalizing Greek and Turkish affairs, the departments of State and Defense had failed to keep the U.S. delegation in Athens informed of either the pace or the key components of the negotiations going on in Ankara. The projected Turkish aid figures were as rude a shock to the American as to the Greek negotiators who, as it happened, were touring defense plants in the United States when the announcement was made.

Prime Minister Karamanlis reacted to the news from Ankara by immediately suspending the Greek DECA negotiations and recalling his delegation from the United States. He informed the head of the U.S. delegation that Greece would be formulating new demands for military assistance in light of the Turkish DECA's aid provisions. He then instructed the Greek Foreign Ministry to come up with new figures. This involved a comparison of aggregate U.S. military assistance to Greece and Turkey since 1947. When the Foreign Ministry compared the figures on Turkish aid it received from the Greek embassy in Ankara with its own record of aid to Greece in the same period, the 7 : 10 ratio emerged. The Karamanlis government promptly demanded that a $700-million military aid package be included in the Greek DECA. When the Ford administration had verified the Greek figures, Secretary of State Kissinger approved a commitment to seek this amount from Congress. Negotiations were resumed, and a new DECA was initialed in July 1977, although, for reasons we will discuss later, it was never signed. The 7 : 10 ratio has since remained the unofficial but authoritative definition of "Aegean balance" to the Greek government. Despite assertions by Athens that 7 : 10 is an obligation embodied in U.S. law, the ratio is not spelled out in any legislation. Since 1978, the executive branch has made a point of submitting aid requests that diverge from 7 : 10, and Congress has just as regularly restored the ratio by reducing the Turkish total and/or adding to the Greek. Not the least of the ironies implicit in this ritual is that it puts administrations in the position of forgoing a rare congressional offer to appropriate funds on strictly political grounds— something the executive has solicited in other circumstances— and Congress in the position of voluntarily surrendering its authority—jealously guarded as a rule—to evaluate aid submissions on their merits.

Executive branch objections to 7 : 10 do not arise from a concern to protect congressional prerogatives. They reflect instead the realization that if Greek aid is pegged at 70 percent of Turkish aid, the extremely large amounts of assistance the administration believes to be needed by Turkey will be impossible to obtain. This has proved to be the case every year since the embargo was lifted—at least until the time of this writing, when Congress, influenced by Turkey's key contribution to military victory in the gulf war, seemed ready to set 7 : 10 aside temporarily for FY 1992. The ratio has been maintained by Congress up to the present at levels significantly lower than those sought by the administration. In FY 1988, for example, Turkish disappointment over a total aid appropriation of $525.3, reduced by Congress from an administration request for $913.5 million, led to a temporary decision by the Turkish government to suspend ratification of the letters it had exchanged with the United States in March 1987 extending the DECA through the end of 1990.

Another reason for the distaste with which the executive branch views 7 : 10 is the belief of policymakers that the ratio "is an artificial judgement which distorts the fundamental facts of Turkish needs and NATO-U.S. interests in meeting these. . . . Assistance should be provided to both Greece and Turkey in accordance with their own particular NATO-related requirements, without regard to any mechanical ratio between allies."[5] The logic of this statement is irrefutable, but it would be more convincing if the executive branch had not in so many other cases permitted political considerations to determine aid levels. The requirements of Israel and Egypt, the recipients of the largest amounts of U.S. military aid since 1979, are certainly being judged by criteria that are no less political. Even within the NATO family, political factors have played an important role in deciding who gets what and in what proportion. The most questionable hypothesis underlying our Greek and Turkish aid programs is not the ratio, which, after all, reflects the reality of their troubled relations, but the pretence that we have been arming them against an outside threat rather than against each other.

It is, in fact, arguable that the ratio is an all-purpose bureaucratic device that serves everyone's interests, even those of the

Turks. It spares the executive branch the ordeal of negotiating a new ratio every year and then explaining to the Greeks and their congressional allies how it preserves "the present balance of military strength among countries of the region." It permits the Greek government to appease the concerns of Greek public opinion and prevents U.S. military aid to Turkey from becoming an explosive political issue in Greece. It provides Congress with a reassuring rationale for respective aid levels to Turkey and Greece, which would otherwise provoke sharp domestic controversy, and a rationale for limiting overall levels of aid. It enables the administration to blame Congress when its "best efforts" fail to obtain projected amounts of aid for Turkey, and the Turks to justify tight control of U.S. military activities by blaming the administration when aid falls short of levels that Congress would have been unlikely to approve anyway.

Everyone, in other words, has a politically expedient excuse for doing the politically expedient thing. It is hard to avoid the conclusion that if the Greeks had not invented 7 : 10, someone else would have had to do so. The device is so logical and serviceable, in fact, that even should Congress agree to break 7 : 10 in response to special circumstances, like the gulf war, it is safe to assume that the ratio will return as long as Greece and Turkey remain at swords' points and Cyprus remains divided.

This does not dispose of the argument that the military needs of Turkey and Greece as members of NATO, the needs, that is, which must be filled if they are to possess a credible defensive capability against a third party, cannot be determined by a ratio designed to measure their defensive capabilities against each other. It does suggest, however, that the best way to eliminate 7 : 10 is to eliminate the conditions that created it. As long as we are unwilling to develop a policy toward Greece and Turkey that promotes real regional balance by helping them find long-term solutions to their bilateral problems, we are better off with the ratio than without it.

To judge from the erratic fluctuations in military aid levels to Greece and Turkey in the years before 1978, when Congress adopted 7 : 10, we might be better off with a ratio under any circumstances. As we have seen, 7 : 10 was deduced by the

Greeks from a comparison of *aggregate* U.S. military aid totals from 1946 to 1976. The ratio actually conceals the inconsistency of our aid policies from year to year and the extent to which they have been influenced by factors other than Greece's and Turkey's "particular NATO-related requirements." During the period when Greek governments were battling a Communist-led guerrilla insurgency, and in the years immediately following the Communists' defeat—from FY 1947 to FY 1951—the ratio was two- or three-to-one in favor of Greece.[6] Between FY 1952 and FY 1964, the ratio shifted toward Turkey, although in FY 1953 it was 8:10 and in FY 1960 11:10 for no obvious military reason.[7] In FYs 1964, 1965, and 1966 the ratio again approached 10:10,[8] and in the seven years of the Greek junta, from FY 1967 through FY 1974, when a partial embargo on arms shipments to Greece was in effect, the ratio tilted toward Turkey,[9] only to be reversed in favor of Greece during the years of the Turkish embargo, from FY 1977 through FY 1979.[10] Since FY 1980, Congress has maintained the 7 : 10 ratio with a precision that owed more to political than to strategic or even mathematical calculations. In FY 1988, for example, military aid to Greece was 70 percent of military aid to Turkey; in FY 1989, it was 70.06 percent; and in FYs 1990 and 1991, again exactly 70 percent.

It is apparent from the foregoing data that for a period of 27 years, from FY 1952, when Greece and Turkey entered NATO, through FY 1979, there was little predictability in the Greek and Turkish military aid programs due to shifting criteria and priorities in both the executive and legislative branches. For the seven years of the Greek junta, from 1967 to 1974, and the three-and-a-half years of the Turkish arms embargo from 1975 to 1978, military aid to both countries was limited by factors unrelated to NATO requirements. The case for limiting aid in these periods was perfectly respectable—indeed, for anyone who believes that NATO should practice what it preaches, impeccable—but it refutes the claim that 7 : 10 has distorted a process of aid allocation that would otherwise by governed exclusively by the military needs of the alliance.

In girding itself for the unknown perils of the future, what the NATO alliance needs more than new and larger amounts of military hardware on its southeastern flank is a restored political consensus that permits Greek and Turkish agreement on their roles, missions, and respective military priorities within NATO and leads to their active cooperation. Just as competitive relationships with the United States have encouraged Athens and Ankara to negotiate more with Washington than with each other, the unpredictability of military aid supplies over the years, and the inconsistent way in which the United States applied political criteria before 1978,[11] have led Greece and Turkey to view the congressional aid hearings from the standpoint of lobbyists, not allies. They have, if anything, become overly sensitized to the executive-legislative balance of power, seeking sometimes to enhance their bargaining position in Washington even at the expense of NATO's deterrent credibility. This was certainly the case when Greece withdrew from the military structure of NATO in August 1974, in protest against the failure of the United States and NATO to react effectively when Turkish forces on Cyprus greatly expanded the perimeter of their beachhead. The same can be said of Turkey's refusal in September 1979 to grant without prior Soviet concurrence overflight rights for U.S. U-2 aircraft based in Cyprus, which were needed for SALT II verification.

In a variation of this kind of maneuvering, Greece and Turkey have, on occasion, become so preoccupied with the tactical complexities of the U.S. legislative process that they have been willing to sacrifice tangible material gains for supposed positional advantages, a gambit even riskier in diplomacy than in chess. Examples could be gleaned from many periods, but one of the clearest is the failure of Turkey and Greece to sign advantageous defense and economic cooperation agreements with the United States in 1976 and 1977, each fearing that the other was getting a better deal. It was the Greeks who began the process.

The climate for negotiating a defense agreement with the United States was especially favorable to Greece in February 1975, when negotiations began. The United States was conscious of having failed to distance itself sufficiently from the Greek military regime that had fallen the previous summer. At the same time, we had coped incompetently with the Cyprus crisis, in part because of failure to assess it accurately, in part because the Nixon administration was incapable of a major diplomatic initiative in its final weeks. As negotiations with the Greeks began, we were also faced with the imminent collapse of noncommunist governments in Vietnam and Cambodia and with them, the last vestiges of our Southeast Asia policy. Altogether, it had been a bad year for U.S. foreign policy and particularly for our policy toward Greece. An important objective of the DECA negotiations, therefore, was to restore Greek confidence in U.S. leadership of the Western alliance and demonstrate our good will toward the political government of Constantine Karamanlis, who had come to power in a landslide victory three months earlier.

The text of the 1977 DECA has not been released, but we know[12] that it included a $700-million military aid package, spread over four years; a carefully hedged but not insignificant security guarantee, framed in the form of an exchange of letters between Kissinger and the Greek foreign minister, Dimitri Bitsios; and assurances that the Greek government would obtain on terms no less favorable than other allies (i.e., Turkey) certain scarce items of military equipment in which the Greeks were at that time especially interested, mainly because they understood similar concessions had been made to the Turks. The equipment included AWACS, enchanced anti-aircraft ground defenses, and surplus F-4 and F-5E aircraft. There were also provisions covering training and intelligence-sharing that were extremely favorable to the Greeks.

Measuring the 1977 DECA against agreements with other allies negotiated in the same period reveals it to be among the most concessionary offered by the United States, comparable to the Turkish DECA negotiated in 1976 but with the added premium of the Kissinger-Bitsios letter. The Greeks, however, were more intent on denying concessions to the Turks than in gaining something for themselves. They feared that the signing and implementation of their 1977 DECA would cause Congress to activate the 1976 Turkish DECA by removing the arms embargo levied in 1975. Lobbying energetically behind the scenes against lifting the embargo, the Greeks delayed cashing in on their own agreement. They miscalculated. The embargo was lifted in September 1978, and a new round of maneuvering between Greece and Turkey began.

The Turks, who had been satisfied enough with the terms of their own DECA in 1976, now believed that its assistance provisions were inadequate. They argued that Turkey deserved compensation for military equipment promised but not received in FYs 1977 and 1978 because of the embargo. They also complained that the U.S. offer of $700 million over four years to Greece implied agreement with the Greek contention that Turkey posed a military threat. The 7 : 10 ratio, including Turkish attempts to break it and Greek attempts to sustain it, had made its first appearance, although it is doubtful that the Turks suspected the magical properties it would acquire subsequently in the eyes of the Greeks.

For these reasons, the Turks deferred formal acceptance of the 1976 DECA, causing the Greeks, who feared new U.S. concessions to Turkey, to procrastinate again. Washington, for its part, was in no hurry to implement agreements that in general created operating conditions less favorable to the U.S. than the ones they replaced. Negotiations with the Turks were resumed and a new DECA was signed in March 1980, projecting larger amounts of aid and committing the United States to use its "best efforts"[13] to obtain them from Congress. The Greeks were then ready to resume negotiations, fortified by their knowledge of what was in the new Turkish agreement. When they at last sat down to talk in 1980, they found, however, that the U.S. position had hardened in the interim. Instead of being willing to amplify the terms of the 1977 agreement, the U.S. delegation made it clear that Washington did not consider itself bound by terms the Greeks had never formally accepted. Athens was faced with a tougher negotiation in 1980 than in 1975 under less favorable circumstances. In the end, no agreement was reached, and when negotiations began again in 1982 they were with a new Greek government with sharply different views of what it wanted in the way of military cooperation with the United States.

The maneuvering of Greece and Turkey for advantage over each other, like the institutionalization of 7 : 10, was encouraged by U.S. policies that lacked predictability and in the period of the Cold War focused so exclusively on the Soviet military threat that they were no help in distinguishing anything else. Greece and Turkey became lobbyists, and remain so today, even as the original U.S. justification for arming them to the teeth has vanished. The executive and legislative branches of the U.S. government, and even agencies within the branches, are also drawn into the Greek-Turkish contest. Anyone who has dealt in Washington with Aegean problems—or with Cyprus—knows that the so-called Greek lobby is only the best known of a variety of special interest groups that concern themselves, often passionately, with Greek-Turkish problems. It is often said, to explain the existence of 7 : 10, that there are more Greek than Turkish Americans. But the depth of feeling of those who believe that Turkey is a loyal ally which has been getting a raw deal is suggested by the title of a recent book, *Turkey: America's Forgotten Ally*,[14] an epithet applied with difficulty to a country which since 1947 has been a leading recipient of U.S. military and economic aid and has consistently been cast by Washington to play a pivotal role in the security of the region.

In Congress, the influence of politically articulate Greek Americans in upholding 7 : 10 against challenges by the executive branch counterbalances rather than unbalances the instinctive bias of policymakers, whatever the administration, who are inclined to think in global or regional rather than subregional terms and are bound to calculate the return on military aid in terms of what it will produce in the form of trained soldiery, up-to-strength divisions, operational facilities, and modern weapons deployed within range of lucrative targets. Turkey, by these standards, is unlikely to be overlooked, much less forgotten.[15] Thanks in part to congressional jogging of the executive branches' institutional memory, neither, for that matter, is Greece, although its strategic displacement is not commensurate with that of Turkey.[16]

But our single-minded attention to the military capabilities of Turkey and Greece, and our neglect of the political and economic context that determines how those capabilities can be used, continue to produce brittle relations and wooden policies:

the Jupiter missile decision, the making and unmaking of home-porting, the Dulles and Johnson letters, 7 : 10, and many more. By continuing to regard Greek-Turkish problems as an annoying distraction from our main business of military security, we deny ourselves the ability to develop realistic, well-rounded policies that will enable Greece and Turkey once again to play an effective role as allies rather than lobbyists and to build a healthier, stronger relationship with them both.

4

THE SOVIET AND MIDDLE EAST CONNECTIONS: BARRIERS AND STEPPING STONES

Among its other strategic implications, the Persian Gulf crisis of 1990–1991 was a reminder of the importance of Turkey, Greece, and Cyprus as states whose land, sea, and air spaces command the western approaches to the Middle East. Without the full cooperation of Turkey, the economic embargo of Iraq would have lacked credibility even as an admonition, and the military campaign would almost certainly have been more drawn out and costly. It is estimated that between 5 and 10 percent of U.S. air strikes against Iraq were launched from bases in Turkey, a relatively small number, but one that probably exceeds the number of strike sorties flown by the entire U.S. navy during the course of the war.[1] In addition, Turkish cooperation with the U.S.–led military coalition, and Ankara's reinforcement of its troops along the Iraqi border, deprived Saddam Hussein of a sanctuary to his rear and forced him to allow for the possibility of a two-front ground war.

The Greek contribution to the defeat of Iraq was less dramatic and less publicized—in part, because the opposition parties to the left of the Greek government succeeded in putting Prime Minister Constantine Mitsotakis on the defensive and caused him to downplay the Greek role at home—but was valuable, especially to the Western Europeans, who used NATO bunkering and other support facilities on the island of Crete, as well as Greek air space, to sustain their military effort. It is also likely that electronic intelligence-collecting facilities on Greek soil were utilized to the advantage of the coalition. In the case of Cyprus, the British sovereign base areas (SBAs) would have been indispensable to British forces and almost certainly also benefited Britain's allies.

The perception of Greece, Turkey, and Cyprus either as stepping stones or barriers to gaining access to the Middle East has been prominent in the minds of U.S. policymakers from the very beginning of our security relationship. It was the paramount reason for inviting Greece and Turkey to join NATO in 1952 and contributed to Washington's ambivalence toward the idea of any change in the status of Cyprus as a British Crown colony before 1960. In the climate of the early 1950s, it was of course their potential role as barriers to Soviet expansion into the Middle East that made them seem so essential to our policy of containment. It is worth recalling that when U.S. chiefs of mission from Middle Eastern posts met in Istanbul in February 1951 and unanimously advocated a formal security arrangement with Greece and Turkey, preferably through NATO membership, they said that it would contribute "to our main goal . . . to prevent the USSR from gaining control of any of the Middle East countries by subversion or other means short of war."[2]

This Middle Eastern connection is still frequently cited in U.S. public statements and in congressional testimony as one of the principal justifications for large military aid programs in Turkey and, to a lesser extent, Greece. Until the gulf war, however, the actual support offered by Greece and Turkey to U.S. policy in the Middle East was scant and had declined progressively since 1951. The hope that their NATO membership would help discourage Soviet takeovers "by subversion and other means short of war" had proved as exaggerated as the threat itself. Both the United States and the Soviet Union saw clients and special relationships come and go in the area. Aside from its firm but unwritten commitment to the continued existence of Israel, the United States has no military allies in a formal sense in the Middle East, and the Soviet Union has never acquired them outside the Warsaw Pact, except for North Korea. Greece and Turkey have defined their own arm's-length relations with Israel—in the case of Greece, not extending de jure recognition until 1990—and have made it clear that any operational use of U.S. facilities for non-NATO purposes must be specifically authorized by them, that is, by two states which believe they have more to gain from the Arabs than from the Israeli's.

Now that Soviet and U.S. Middle Eastern policies have become less antagonistic and Turkey and Greece have capitalized on their geographic position to hasten a coalition victory in the gulf war, we will hear less about them as barriers and more about them as stepping stones. Policy differences with respect to Israel's position in the Middle East still exist between Washington and Moscow, and may well be sharpened when Arabs and Israelis begin serious peace negotiations, but Soviet fears—and U.S. expectations—that were aroused when Greece and Turkey joined NATO have diminished as it has become increasingly clear that Greece and Turkey are pursuing their own policies in the area and that these are as compatible with Moscow's priorities as with Washington's.

Greece and Turkey, nevertheless, have real and enduring strategic importance for the Soviet Union. The reason is clear from a look at the map. They lie directly athwart Soviet sea and air lines of communication (LOCs) to the Mediterranean and beyond; they offer vantage points to the United States and NATO for electronic reconnaissance and surveillance, especially from eastern Turkey and the Greek island of Crete; and their military collaboration potentially enhances NATO's maneuverability in the eastern Mediterranean and limits that of the Soviet Union. Since it has been estimated that between 70 and 80 percent of the USSR's supplies to Vladivostok are shipped via the Mediterranean and that, according to one U.S. expert, "over 60% of its exports go through the Bosphorus and an average of 150 Soviet merchant ships ride the Mediterranean at any one time,"[3] it is clear that the Soviets will continue to pay close attention to their southern LOC's. There are, in other words, permanent Soviet interests in the area as vital to President Gorbachev's foreign policy as they were to that of his predecessors, however differently he chooses to express and pursue them. Gorbachev indicated as much publicly during his first visit to the United States.

One of the most interesting and least noted comments by the Soviet leader in the course of his long Washington press conference of December 10, 1987, dealt with NATO's southern flank. Addressing the balance of conventional forces then existing in Europe, Gorbachev observed that "those who speak of [the Warsaw Pact's advantage on the central front] . . . gloss over in silence the fact that NATO has an immense superiority on the southern flank of Europe, next to the borders of our country, the Soviet Union."[4] Since the prevailing view of Western military experts at that time conceded the Soviets and their allies a clear land- and air-power advantage in the southeastern theater, Gorbachev was evidently referring to the tactical edge of the U.S. Sixth Fleet, a point he underlined three months later in Belgrade when he referred to the Mediterranean as "an intricate knot of conflicting interests abounding in huge military arsenals" and proposed a freeze on U.S. and Soviet fleet strength, to be followed by the imposition of naval ceilings and the eventual withdrawal of superpower warships.[5]

This proposal, doubtless intended more to stimulate anti-Sixth Fleet sentiment in Yugoslavia than as a serious diplomatic initiative, is nevertheless an authoritative reminder that, even after the Cold War, the Soviet Union will continue to seek ways to protect its interests in the Mediterranean basin, just as the United States and its Western European allies will continue to do so. The objectives of the Soviets in this region have been remarkably constant. Since World War II, they have chosen to emphasize different aspects of their Mediterranean policy at different times, abandoning tactics that proved unproductive and adopting new ones, but their main goals have been entirely consistent with the historic Russian need to secure by diplomatic and military means unhindered access to the Mediterranean and relief from the threat of invasion from the south.

The fundamental change that has occurred in the climate of East-West relations since 1986 means, first, that when Soviet interests conflict with those of the United States, as they continue to on such questions as U.S. military facilities in Greece and Turkey and British sovereign base areas in Cyprus, there will be less linkage with other issues and less damage to overall relations; and, second, that on some questions, like unimpeded navigation in the Aegean, the Soviets will work actively with us to secure shared objectives.

One striking example of such cooperation took place in 1988 in the context of the Vienna negotiations to reduce conventional forces in Europe (CFE). Greek-Turkish differences had obtruded on these talks whenever NATO representatives discussed the geographic zones that would be subject to CFE controls and inspection. The Greek position was that the Turkish port of Mersin, from which Turkish troops in northern Cyprus are provisioned from the Anatolian mainland, must be included in the zone affected by CFE agreements. Their position was reliably supported by the Soviets who understandably favored any extension of CFE controls in NATO countries and, with particular enthusiasm, an extension proposed by one NATO state at the expense of another. As long as the conventional arms talks were being conducted with no sense of urgency, the Mersin issue was only a minor irritant that could be put aside while issues of greater importance to European security were discussed.

As U.S.-Soviet relations improved under the influence of *glasnost* and *perestroika,* and when new possibilities for agreement on strategic arms became unmistakable after the October 1986 summit meeting between Ronald Reagan and Mikhail Gorbachev in Reykjavik, the prospects for reducing conventional arms began to look much more promising. The U.S. president and his Soviet counterpart had placed arms control at the top of the U.S.-Soviet agenda, and both were now committed to progress in all categories of weapons and forces.

Throughout 1987, the focus was on nuclear weapons, culminating in the signature of the Washington INF treaty in December, eliminating all land-based intermediate-range nuclear missiles. By the beginning of 1988, the attention of the U.S. and Soviet leadership had turned to conventional forces. In March, NATO heads of state called for renewed efforts to eliminate conventional force disparities. In May, the beginning of Soviet troop withdrawals from Afghanistan further improved the climate for reaching conventional arms agreements.

In this new atmosphere, with the United States and the Soviet Union manifestly serious about reducing conventional forces in Europe, the Mersin issue suddenly assumed real importance. Without the concurrence of Greece and Turkey, no agreed-upon NATO position could be presented to the Soviets. Greek-Turkish differences had become a major obstacle to East-West agreement, and it was clearly incumbent on the United States to bring its two NATO allies into line. Repeated attempts to work out a compromise with them behind the scenes failed. The Republic of Cyprus was as adamant as Greece that Mersin must be included in the zone subject to CFE controls. In these circumstances, the Soviet Union might have been expected to let Washington sort out the problem if it could and, if it could not, blame the Americans and NATO for failure to reach an agreement.

Instead, to the vast discomfiture of Greece and the Republic of Cyprus, the Soviets changed their position and declared they would no longer insist on the inclusion of Mersin in the CFE zone. The Greeks and the Cypriots found themselves in the awkward position of being pressured by *both* the Soviets and the Americans to withdraw their objections to the exclusion of Mersin. The extraordinary outcome of the affair was that a formula of words was devised—by the Soviets!—that defined the Turkish zone ambiguously enough to enable the Turks to assert that Mersin was excluded and the Greeks to assert that it was not.[6]

As long as the Soviet Union attaches primary importance to reaching agreement with the United States on such overarching issues as conventional arms control, Moscow will share American impatience when Greek-Turkish differences seem to be obstructing the process of accommodation. Having proved willing in the case of Mersin to work out a settlement between two NATO allies—after the United States had tried and failed—there should be other occasions in the future when the Soviets will work with us to address specific Greek-Turkish disputes that adversely affect interests we have in common.

Cyprus may be one of these. Even before the Cold War ended, Soviet policy toward Cyprus was generally low-keyed. At first glance, it would have been logical to assume that Soviet interests in the eastern Mediterranean would best be served by stirring up as much trouble as possible between Greeks and Turks and letting NATO take the heat. The Soviet Union, after all, was often accused in the West of "fishing in troubled waters," and few waters have been more troubled since 1955 than those around Cyprus.

Yet, after Cypriot independence in 1960, Soviet policy was anything but adventurous. It expressed consistent support for the republic's nonaligned status and avoided major interventions in Cypriot affairs. The Communist parties of Cyprus, Greece, and Turkey—the latter illegal but as faithful a purveyor of the Moscow line as the other two—have been consistent advocates of détente between Greece and Turkey, far more outspoken in this regard than their non-Communist opponents.[7]

Security considerations have evidently been the decisive influence on Soviet policy. Particularly after the Turkish Cypriots unilaterally declared the establishment of the Turkish Republic of Northern Cyprus in November 1983, an important Soviet concern has been to prevent the present de facto partition of Cyprus from becoming permanent, a development they fear might lead to the union of northern Cyprus with Turkey and the establishment of U.S. or NATO bases there. For similar reasons, the Soviets have sought the elimination of the British sovereign base areas at Akrotiri and Dhekelia, calling for the withdrawal of all foreign troops "from the island," as opposed to their withdrawal from the republic—which would imply acceptance of the SBAs. In Cyprus, therefore, although the United States and the Soviet Union approach the problem from different directions, there is shared concern about the inherent instability of present arrangements and, consequently, shared incentive to work together to improve them. We will look more closely in chapter 9 at the implications of convoking an international conference on the Cyprus problem, as advocated by the Soviet Union, Greece, and the Republic of Cyprus.

While the improved climate of East-West relations opens up new approaches to Greek-Turkish problems through U.S.-Soviet cooperation, it would be unrealistic to expect future Soviet governments to abandon the pursuit of strategic objectives in the Mediterranean that run counter to Western interests and have, in some cases, been constant since the days of the tsars. In the past, Soviet objectives included the following: to promote a regime on the Bosphorus and the Dardanelles that facilitated military and civilian passage by Soviet vessels and impeded that of other powers, especially non-Black Sea powers; to neutralize the military value of Turkey to any potential adversary of the Soviet Union; to maintain freedom of passage through the Aegean and discourage the Greeks from extending their territorial sea to twelve miles; to support Bulgarian aspirations for an outlet to the Aegean; and to obtain expanded use of Turkish air space for Soviet combat and transport aircraft en route to the Middle East and North Africa.

Not all Soviet objectives are antithetical to those espoused by the United States and NATO—who, as we have seen, are just as interested as the Soviet Union in maintaining freedom of navigation in the Aegean and have no real desire to change the non-aligned status of Cyprus—but their unifying purpose since World War II has been to free the Soviets from the constraints that NATO placed on them when Greece and Turkey became alliance members in 1952, and NATO's maritime flank advanced east 1,000 miles from the Adriatic to the Gulf of Iskenderun.

In anticipating how the Soviets will react in the future to conflicts of interest in the Aegean and Cyprus, as well as how helpful they can be when our interests are complementary, we need to assess the effectiveness of their past policies in the region and whether they have been more skillful than we in conducting their relations with Greece, Turkey, and Cyprus. Let us first examine Soviet relations with Turkey. Three periods reveal three contrasting approaches to an issue vital to Soviet security, namely, naval passage between the Black Sea and the Mediterranean. The first is that leading up the Montreux Convention of 1936; the second is that of the Nazi-Soviet pact between 1938 and 1941; and the third is the time immediately following World War II.

The Montreux Convention was negotiated upon the initiative of the Turks, who were dissatisfied with the demilitarization of the Dardanelles and the limited authority entrusted to them over military traffic by the Lausanne Treaty of 1923. Their desire to revise military portions of the Straits Convention was supported by the Soviet Union, which Turkey had been the first power to recognize after the Bolshevik revolution and which had concluded a treaty of friendship and nonaggression with Turkey in 1925. Turkey's desire to gain more control over military traffic through the straits coincided, therefore, with the Soviet Union's desire to limit the naval presence of nonlittoral states in the Black Sea. The new regime negotiated at Montreux permitted Turkey to militarize the straits and, more important, empowered the Turks to control military traffic in accordance with strict guidelines affecting clearance and tonnage. In exchange for a measure of relief from the threat of an unfriendly naval presence on their southern flank, the Soviets accepted conditions affecting passage of their own warships through the straits that, in the changed situation after World War II, particularly when Turkey joined NATO, became inconvenient to them, and today, even with a relaxed Turkish attitude, limit their surge capability and the speed and secrecy with which they can make naval deployments in the Mediterranean.[8]

Relief from the restrictions of the straits regime established at Montreux was one of the enticements used by Adolf Hitler in 1940 when he wished to convince the Soviets of his desire to bring them into the Axis. Documents from the archives of the German Foreign Office summarize a pertinent exchange between Hitler[9] and V. M. Molotov on November 13, 1940: "To a question by Molotov regarding the German position on the question of the Straits, the Fuhrer replied that the Reich Foreign Minister had already considered this point and that he had envisioned a revision of the Montreux Convention in favor of the Soviet Union."[10] Hitler later in the same conversation stated that Molotov's views on a revision of the Montreux Convention "would conform approximately with Germany's views, according to which only Russian warships might pass freely through the Dardanelles, while the Straits would be closed to all other warships. . . . "[11]

After Molotov's return to Moscow, where he reported to Stalin on his discussions in Berlin, the Soviets elaborated their concerns in terms consistent with their continuing objectives in the Mediterranean. The German ambassador outlined the Soviet conditions for joining the Axis in a telegram (classified "Strictly Secret") sent to Berlin on November 26, 1940. These were: the conclusion of a mutual assistance pact with Bulgaria to "assure the security of the Soviet Union in the Straits" and the "establishment of a base for land and naval forces of the USSR within range of the Bosphorus and the Dardanelles by means of a long-term lease"; recognition that "the area south of Batum and Baku in the general direction of the Persian Gulf is . . . the center of the aspirations of the Soviet Union"; a draft protocol on Turkey to "guarantee a base for light naval and air and land forces of the USSR on the Bosphorus and the Dardanelles by means of a long-term lease, including—in case Turkey declares herself willing to join the Four Power Pact—a guarantee of the independence and territorial integrity of Turkey by the three countries named (Germany, Italy, the USSR)."[12] It is noteworthy that in discussing the proposed pact with Bulgaria, Molotov informed Hitler that "Russia was prepared to guarantee Bulgaria an outlet to the Aegean Sea,"[13] meaning a port in eastern (Greek) Macedonia, which Bulgaria had already occupied twice in the twentieth century and was destined to occupy a third time from 1941 to 1944.

As World War II neared its end, with the defeat of the Axis assured, and allied consultations at Yalta (in February 1945) and Potsdam (in July and August) increasingly concerned with patterns of postwar collaboration, the Soviet Union changed tactics and abandoned its conciliatory policies of the 1920s and 1930s. Having already signaled its dissatisfaction with the existing straits regime at Yalta, the Soviet government in March 1945 denounced its 1925 treaty of friendship and nonaggression with Turkey (which it had renewed in 1941) and in June called for joint Soviet-Turkish defense of the straits and the installation there of Soviet bases. These demands were coupled with another seeking rectification of the Soviet-Turkish border in the Caucasus and cession of the eastern Turkish provinces of Kars and Ardahan to the Soviet Union.

The sudden hardening of the Soviet line toward Turkey, which more or less coincided with the start of the third round of fighting between Greek government forces, supported by the British, and Communist guerrillas, who the West believed were supported by Moscow, helped convince London and Washington that a major Soviet diplomatic and paramilitary offensive was being launched against Turkey and Greece. The Truman Doctrine was not announced until March 1947, but the Cold War had begun two years earlier.

The fact that it began when Soviet pressure was applied (indirectly) on Greece and (directly) on Turkey—at a time when the Soviet Union was also attempting to establish a puppet regime in Iranian Azerbaijan—underlines the importance attached by the Soviets to their southern flank. Moscow's concerns, moreover, were not exclusively defensive in the immediate postwar period and did not stop at the Dardanelles. In light of later and persistent Soviet attempts to secure land-based naval support facilities in the Mediterranean, it is interesting to recall that Molotov, in September 1945, sought a Soviet trusteeship over Tripolitania, a demand scaled down in January 1946 to joint Soviet-Italian administration. Failure to gain this objective caused the Soviets to delay approving the transfer of the Dodecanese islands from Italy to Greece until 1946.[14]

Soviet tactics changed again in 1953, after the death of Stalin, when the Soviets retracted their territorial claim to Turkey's eastern provinces and disclaimed any desire to revise the straits regime. There were sharp Soviet protests and propaganda blasts when Turkey signed the Balkan Pact with Greece and Yugoslavia in 1953, joined CENTO in 1955, signed a defense agreement with the United States in 1959, and accepted Jupiter intermediate-range missiles in 1960, but post-Stalin policies have shown the Soviets to be aware that direct or implied military threats against Ankara have not worked to their advantage. The evident uncertainty of the Soviets about what kind of policies will work better, and the muffled quality of their pronouncements on bilateral issues in dispute between Greece and Turkey, including some, like Law of the Sea questions, in which they have an independent interest, suggest that "Aegean balance" has become almost as difficult a problem for Moscow as it is for Washington.

The Soviets betray the same inconsistency in their relations with Greece where, for geographic reasons, Russian interests are less exposed, although trouble in the Aegean can affect Soviet shipping in its most important southern waterway. As in the case of Turkey, Soviet policy has fluctuated between threats and blandishments, with many indications that the Soviet leadership lacks familiarity with Greek psychology and is baffled by the apparent imperviousness of Greeks, including Greek Communists, to "objective" factors.[15] Soviet support after 1945 for the Communist guerrilla fighters in the Greek civil war, which Britain and the United States thought was masterminded by Moscow, we now know to have been equivocal. In his meeting with Winston Churchill in Moscow in October 1944, Stalin had, in effect, consigned Greece to the Western sphere of influence. By 1948, immediately before his break with Marshal Tito, Stalin is quoted by the dissident Yugoslav leader, Milovan Djilas, as calling for the Communist-led guerrilla war against the Greek government to be "folded up."[16] In the summer of 1949 it was. Soviet policy toward Greece after that time was no clearer or more consistent than it was toward Turkey, varying from Nikita Khrushchev's bluster in 1961 that the Soviets, if they chose, could level the Acropolis, to Greek-Soviet summitry in 1979, when Prime Minister Karamanlis visited Moscow.

While the prevailing trend in Soviet policy since the fall of the Greek junta in 1974 has been toward better relations with Athens, Moscow has been as careful to avoid offending the Turks in its actions and statements as Washington has. More so, if we recall such U.S. initiatives as the Johnson letter of 1964; the Kissinger-Bitsios letter of 1976[17] (which bothered Ankara enough to cause Secretary of State Alexander Haig five years later to respond to Greek press queries about its validity by saying only that the letter was "in the files";[18] and the wording of the preamble to the 1990 Defense and Economic Cooperation Agreement[19] between the United States and Greece (which provoked strong Turkish government protests to Washington).

By contrast, the Soviets have generally refrained from public statements that could be interpreted to refer to bilateral issues in dispute between Greece and Turkey. When Soviet premier Nikolai Tikhonov paid a state visit to Athens in February 1983, for example, the Papandreou government, which prided itself on following what might be described as a nonaligned policy within NATO, and which had already declared its support for the Kremlin-sponsored concept of a Balkan nuclear-free zone—which Turkey opposed—clearly anticipated a reciprocal gesture in the form of an expression of Soviet concern about tensions in the Aegean. Athens had recently charged that Turkish (and U.S.) aircraft were violating Greek air space in the course of military exercises. Greek government newspapers had reported confidently that Soviet support for the Greek position would be expressed in the communiqué to be issued at the conclusion of the Tikhonov visit. When the communiqué was released, the Soviet portion not only failed to support the Greek position but made no mention of the Aegean at all.

Although Moscow has blown hot and cold in its relations with both Greece and Turkey, the Soviets, as experienced practitioners of realpolitik, have tended to take Turkey more seriously than Greece and to invest more economic resources there. In the past twenty years, Turkey and Greece have each elected governments of the non-Communist left that presented their foreign policy agendas at least partly as a break with the past and sought to capitalize on popular disaffection with U.S. policies. Turkey's Bülent Ecevit in the 1970s and Greece's Andreas Papandreou in the 1980s actively solicited Soviet aid and investment, but with vastly different results. Soviet project assistance to Turkey (which began in 1958 with a $2-million credit for road construction) has financed a steel mill in Iskenderun, an aluminum plant in Seydisehir, a petroleum refinery near Izmir, a fiber-sheet factory in Artvin, as well as power plants, transmission lines, and other projects.[20] Not all of these projects were initiated when Ecevit was in power, and outmoded technology and faulty feasibility studies have made the economic value of many of the projects questionable. Still, during this period Moscow's credits increased to the point that by 1978, according to one estimate, "Turkey had become the largest single recipient of Soviet aid among semi-industrialized countries."[21] Greece by contrast has received credits for the purchase of such things as road-building equipment, Polish firefighting airplanes, and Romanian buses. The only major project that Papandreou announced was a Soviet-financed aluminum plant that had been agreed to in 1979, before the PASOK government came to power. Moscow meanwhile continues to show interest in strengthening economic ties with Turkey. Agreements negotiated with the conservative Özal government for the supply of Soviet natural gas to Turkey will reportedly enable the Turks to offset up to 70 percent of the cost by means of exports to the Soviet Union and construction contracts for Turkish firms. Although Ankara seems to be managing its relationship carefully to avoid overdependency, it is apparent that for the Soviets security considerations—rather than the faint prospects of economic benefits—justify this level of investment in an underdeveloped and inflation-prone NATO country like Turkey. It is, however, hard to discern a consistent pattern in Soviet economic policy. The weakness of the Soviet economy and the shoddiness of most Soviet goods have prevented Moscow from employing trade as an effective instrument of national policy as, for example, Germany did in the 1930s.

The fits and starts of Soviet diplomatic and economic policy are also characteristic of Soviet military policy in the Mediterranean. The strength of the Fifth Eskadra—the Soviet Mediterranean fleet based in the Black Sea—has varied since 1958, when Albania's break with the Soviet Union caused the Soviets to lose their privileges at the submarine base at Valona, and they had for a time no ships regularly patrolling the Mediterranean.[22] The extraordinary growth of the Soviet navy under Adm. Sergei Gorshkov after 1958 brought the Soviet fleet back to the Mediterranean in strength.

"As is seen," wrote Gorshkov in 1972,

> historically it has turned out that when a threat arises of enemy encroachment on the territory of Russia from the southwest, the Russian Navy has been moved into the Mediterranean Sea where it has successfully executed major strategic missions in defending the country's borders from aggression. In other words, our Navy has shown the whole world that the Mediterranean Sea is not anyone's preserve or a closed lake and that Russia is a Mediterranean power. The location of her forces in these waters is based not only on geographical conditions (the proximity of the Black Sea to the Mediterranean theater) but also the age-old need for the Russian Navy to stay there.[23]

The growing presence of the Fifth Eskadra in the Mediterranean under Gorshkov can be seen in numbers of ship days, which increased from only 1,500 per year in 1949 to 19,000 in 1971 and reached a peak of 20,300 in 1973 at the time of the Yom Kippur War. Limited as their sustainability and surge capability have been, especially after Egypt's definitive break with Moscow in 1976, the Soviets have shown that Gorshkov meant what he said. Furthermore, despite its lack of land-based naval support facilities, the Soviet navy in these years improved its sustainability by obtaining better access to ports in Syria, Libya, the Maghreb, and Yugoslavia, developing buoy-marked anchorages in international waters off the Greek islands of Crete and Kythera and points further west, and concluding contracts for repair of Soviet auxiliary vessels in various Mediterranean commercial shipyards, including on the Greek island of Syros.

Between 1977 and 1983, Soviet ship days decreased to under 17,000 per year. Soviet cost-cutting has continued the downward trend and has also resulted in fewer naval exercises in the Mediterranean, as well as in waters farther from home. Figures on ship days naturally also reflect the numbers of fleet units the Fifth Eskadra has deployed to the Mediterranean in given periods. After escalating to a high of 96 units at the time of the Yom Kippur War, the Soviets evidently decided that a smaller naval presence—perhaps 25 units on normal rotation—would do the job. During various Middle Eastern crises since 1973—until the gulf war of 1990–1991—the Fifth Eskadra had about 45 units in the Mediterranean. During the gulf crisis, with the attention of the Soviet government directed toward domestic problems, no increase occurred.[24]

It is unlikely, however, that the Soviets have permanently lost interest in the Eastern Mediterranean. The basic conclusion to be drawn from Soviet naval policy in the region is that whether Moscow is expanding or retrenching its military forces, whether its mood is assertive or retiring, the Soviets will maintain a naval presence in the eastern Mediterranean. As long as the Soviet military and merchant fleet must traverse the Bosphorus and the Turkish straits, passing within sight of the Greek islands of the Aegean en route to the open sea, Turkey and Greece will have an important place in Soviet strategic planning.

The basic conclusion to be drawn from the history of Soviet relations with Greece and Turkey since World War II is that Moscow has shown little more deftness than Washington in its treatment of the Greeks and Turks. Like Washington, Moscow has tried so hard to stay clear of Greek-Turkish problems that effectively exploiting them to the detriment of NATO has been as far beyond the reach of Soviet policy as solving them has been beyond the reach of U.S. policy. That the failures of the Soviets have probably been less costly in terms of their national prestige is simply an indication that less was expected of them by the Greeks and Turks than was expected of their U.S. ally. A more pertinent question is why the Soviets, who should know Greece and Turkey well from long proximity to them, have not done better.

Soviet leaders do not have to plan their policies in four- and eight-year increments, as U.S. administrations do, but they have in the past been just as shortsighted. The often conflicting priorities of the Soviet Foreign Ministry and the Politburo—between the need to conduct state-to-state relations and the need to conduct party-to-party relations—have tended to leach out Soviet foreign policy and make it even more brittle than that of the United States. Needless to say, when conflicts have arisen between the needs of Moscow and those of indigenous Communist parties, the views of Moscow have prevailed. Thus, for decades, the Communist Party of Greece suffered the indignity of having to support the concept of an "independent" Macedonia, favored by the Soviets (and, at different times, by their Yugoslav and Bulgarian allies) and abominated by most Greeks. Similarly, the illegal Communist Party of Turkey, operating from exile in the former German Democratic Republic, was obliged to pay lip service to an independent Kurdistan. These are positions that any knowledgeable Soviet diplomat would have counseled against. The Soviets have trained specialists in Turkish and Greek affairs, especially the former, but their influence was negligible in formulating Soviet policy toward Greece and Turkey during the years of the Cold War. Once again, it is in Cyprus, where the bifurcation between the Communist party's (AKEL) view and Moscow's has been less apparent, and where, accordingly, Soviet policy has been less blurred, that Soviet influence has been most enhanced and where Moscow's cooperation may be most useful in effecting a settlement of existing problems.

Looking at the evolution of Soviet and U.S. relations with Greece and Turkey since 1947, it is one of the ironies of the single-track policies pursued by both the Soviet Union and the United States that their diplomatic stances, which appeared at the time of the Truman Doctrine to foreshadow a major super-power confrontation, are now almost indistinguishable. This may be just as well. The gulf war has demonstrated that Greece, Turkey, and Cyprus have important roles to play in whatever "new world order" emerges in the Middle East. Perhaps the relaxation of tensions between East and West will encourage members of the NATO alliance, working with the Soviet Union where possible, to take a new look at ways they can help Greece and Turkey to resolve their current differences and Cyprus to recover its sovereignty and territorial integrity, under conditions acceptable to both Greek and Turkish Cypriots. Such an effort would be entirely consistent with NATO's expressed desire to become more than a military alliance and to strengthen its political dimension as its military dimension is scaled down.

A more realistic approach by NATO to its southeastern flank is long overdue. The kinds of anodyne communiqué that the North Atlantic Council has issued periodically on Greek-Turkish differences since 1964, when the council first entrusted the secretary general with a "watching brief," have actually contributed to the military problems of the alliance in the eastern Mediterranean by pretending that the political problems are being solved. They are not. And what the secretary general and the alliance have been "watching" all this time is the decomposition of NATO's southeastern flank and the depletion of its own potentially stabilizing influence in the increasingly unstable region of the eastern Mediterranean.

5

ATLANTIC NORTH AND AEGEAN SOUTH: NATO'S WATCHING BRIEF

The late Dimitri Bitsios, Greek foreign minister from 1974 to 1977, explained the withdrawal of Greece from the military command structure of NATO in August 1974 by quoting the words used at the time by Prime Minister Karamanlis, "I had to choose. Either to declare war on Turkey or to leave NATO. Between the two I chose the lesser evil."[1] That the Greek political leader most identified with a policy of Western alignment should have believed it necessary to choose between continued membership in NATO or war against a fellow member demonstrates how far Greek-Turkish antagonism had been permitted to abort the alliance's military mission in the eastern Mediterranean.

The cause of Greek indignation that August was NATO's refusal to play any role in resolving the Cyprus crisis that had exploded in July when an attempt by the military junta then ruling Greece to install an illegal, *enosis*-minded government in Nicosia led to Turkish military intervention. The failure of NATO's secretary-general, Joseph Luns of the Netherlands, on vacation in the Black Forest, to accede to the urgent demand of Athens for an emergency meeting of the North Atlantic Council was particularly galling to the Greeks. After withdrawing from the unified command, six years passed before Greece was nominally reintegrated. The actual terms of Greek reintegration negotiated in Ankara and Athens in 1980 by the supreme allied commander, Gen. Bernard W. Rogers, have still not been implemented.

Greece and Turkey lobby against each other as bitterly in Brussels as they do in Washington and often use the same arguments in disputing NATO's allocation of infrastructure funds that they apply to the apportioning of U.S. military assistance. In 1987 and 1988, for example, their objections to specific projects proposed for infrastructure funding on each other's territory resulted in failure to approve about half of the projects (which require unanimous consent before funds can be disbursed). Since Turkey was scheduled to receive 14 percent and Greece 8 percent of NATO's total infrastructure budget, which amounted to $900 million for the two-year period, the cost to the Turks of failing to unblock the funds—known in NATO jargon as "slices"—was $252 million and to the Greeks $144 million. The disputed projects were located in areas, including the Greek island of Limnos and the Turkish coastline adjacent to it, that are essential to NATO's defense of the straits of the Dardanelles but would be equally significant in the event of Greek-Turkish hostilities. At the time of this writing, in mid-1991, Greece and Turkey are still squabbling over infrastructure funding. In the current NATO budget, slice 42 includes $202 million for Turkey and $130 million for Greece. (For those interested in seeing how NATO stands with respect to 7:10, the ratio for slice 42 is 6.4:10.) Even if the funds are eventually unblocked, delays are costly, and the infrastructure dispute is another example of how failure to address political problems in the Aegean simultaneously damages the interests of Greece and Turkey, who can ill afford to jeopardize funding of this magnitude, and of NATO, which is denied the ability to fortify key salients on its southeastern flank.

The deadlock in NATO has become so implacable that since 1984 Greece and Turkey have even vetoed each other's "national chapters," the yearly inventory of forces assigned to NATO, which serves as a basis for NATO planning and also, in the past, for the alliance's annual "Comparison of NATO and Warsaw Pact Forces," a document that for this reason was not issued after 1984. Much of the secretary-general's diplomatic skill continues to be consumed in deflecting Greek-Turkish differences before they can impede other work of the council. NATO staff officers have learned to spot an Aegean issue on the horizon as quickly as they would have spotted a Soviet Backfire bomber at the height of the Cold War.

If the most obvious benefit NATO gained when Greece and Turkey joined the military organization in 1952 was the opportunity to coordinate a forward defense of its southern flank, its most obvious liability since 1974 has been a lack of coordination that is evident in every forum in which the two allies are represented. Greek and Turkish armed forces do not exercise together regularly, and the last Aegean military exercise conducted by NATO in which Greece permitted its forces to cooperate with Turkey, even on a limited basis, was in the spring of 1982. Most of the exercises that Greece and Turkey have conducted in the Aegean since 1974 have not been against a common adversary but against each other.

The damage to NATO's preparedness, however, goes well beyond this. Greek-Turkish antagonism also disfigures the military structure of the alliance. When Greece withdrew from the unified military command its forces were withdrawn from NATO's regional headquarters in Izmir, Turkey, which accordingly in 1978 became an entirely Turkish command subordinate to the Commander in Chief, Allied Forces, Southern Europe (CINCSOUTH) in Naples. The reintegration of Greek forces worked out by General Rogers envisaged, not the return of the Greeks to Izmir, but the creation of a separate "Greek" NATO headquarters in Larissa, in central Greece, whose projected air arm, the Seventh Allied Tactical Air Force (ATAF), would be the counterpart of the Sixth ATAF in Izmir. Athens and Ankara could not agree, however, on the respective boundaries of the Larissa and Izmir commands, a point that had been left deliberately vague in the reintegration agreement, and the proposed Seventh ATAF has never come into being.

The Greek government insists that NATO members, including the Turks, agree in advance that Larissa's command-and-control authority will correspond with that of the Athens Flight Information Region (FIR), which is to say, will extend over the easternmost Greek islands off the Anatolian coast. The Athens FIR was established in 1952 by the International Civil Aviation Organization (ICAO), after consultation with Greece and Turkey, long before the Cyprus crisis of 1974 and Greece's withdrawal from the NATO unified command. Since then, its validity has been disputed by the Turks.[2] As for the future division of authority between the existing Izmir and the projected Larissa NATO headquarters, Turkey argues that the intent of the Rogers Agreement, accepted by Greece at the time, was that command-and-control lines would be drawn after the Seventh ATAF was established and as a result of negotiations between the Izmir and Larissa commands. The Turkish interpretation is supported by General Rogers.

There is in this debate an element of unreality that characterizes much of the Aegean dispute and NATO's reaction to it. In the first place, it is obvious that Greek-Turkish disagreement is not over the question of when command-and-control lines will be drawn, but where. It is therefore immaterial whether the dispute is resolved before or after the establishment of the Seventh ATAF. From NATO's standpoint, it may even be preferable to resolve the problem before creating the new command in order to avoid the spectacle of two NATO subordinate commands squabbling over their authorities and to end the even worse one of Greek and Turkish fighter pilots playing "chicken" over the Greek islands of the Aegean in the course of NATO exercises.

In the second place, the command-and-control issue is extravagantly theoretical in the absence of actual hostilities. Whatever solution is devised will inevitably give way to the imperatives of the battlefield. It is inconceivable that, under attack from an outside aggressor, Greece would object to air cover directed from Izmir or Turkey from Larissa. The problem would more likely be the perceived insufficiency of allied air support, as it was when Hitler unleashed his offensive against Greece in April 1941. Similarly, it is hard to sustain the position in peacetime that if two allied tactical air forces exist, the Seventh in Greece and the Sixth in Turkey, the Turkish command should be responsible for the defense of Greek territory in the eastern Aegean, a zone where serious bilateral issues remain to be resolved between Greece and Turkey.

The differing Greek and Turkish interpretations of the Rogers Agreement carry Clausewitz's definition of war as a continuation of policy by other means into the realm of military exercises between allies. Athens, ever conscious of Turkey's military strength and the Greek need for "Aegean balance," is particularly sensitive to the legal implications of NATO exercises as they relate to the fortification of Greek islands that Turkey contends must be demilitarized under existing treaty commitments.[3] Until the issue became academic in 1983, when the Papandreou government announced that Greece would no longer participate in allied exercises in the Aegean that excluded the island of Limnos, which the Greeks had militarized over Turkish objections, it was easier to compose an Aegean scenario realistically projecting the capabilities of Warsaw Pact forces in the area than those of Greece and Turkey—which were kept secret from each other and from the alliance.

In the fall of 1983, for example, a scenario was painstakingly negotiated by CINCSOUTH[4] for the Aegean exercise, APEX EXPRESS, which, in deference to Turkish views, omitted Limnos from the exercise area. Given the prominence of Limnos as a terrain feature—it is an island of 186 square miles commanding the southern approaches to the Dardanelles and was significant enough even in antiquity to be occupied by the classical Greeks, the Byzantines, the Genoese, the Venetians, and the Ottomans—its omission from a scenario postulating an attack against Turkish Thrace introduced an element of fantasy into APEX EXPRESS that NATO planners tried to temper by modifying the scenario. They succeeded in persuading the Greek and Turkish general staffs to agree that in the "free play" portion of the exercise, when Greek and Turkish forces were not bound by the scenario, Greek commanders could assume enemy occupation of Limnos and target it for mock bombing runs by the Greek air force. The Greek government could thus assume that Limnos was included in the exercise and the Turkish government that it was not.[5]

That this elaborate charade put the Greeks in the position of targeting their own territory to establish their legal right to defend it may have been too bitter an irony for the Greeks to swallow. The arrangement came unstuck when it was leaked to the Greek press with the (unwarranted) claim that NATO was thereby supporting Greece's right to militarize Limnos. The Turks immediately and publicly objected, and Greece withdrew from the exercise, as it has from all subsequent NATO exercises in the Aegean in which Greek and Turkish forces were scheduled to participate jointly.

The almost total absorption of the Soviet leadership since 1988 in consolidating rather than expanding the power of the Soviet Union, a process that culminated in February 1991 in the formal dissolution of the Warsaw Pact, has made NATO's handling of Greek-Turkish problems less immediately dangerous in military terms but no less illogical. Indeed, if we assume, as the author does, that the dangers of a multipolar world, in which new security systems have yet to be defined, much less tested, make it expedient to preserve and refocus an alliance that has proved its utility, then the need to restore coherence to NATO's southeastern flank has not diminished. The 1990–1991 crisis in the Persian Gulf did not engage NATO forces or facilities in a formal sense (although it might have if Iraqi forces had attacked Turkey), but, as we saw in the last chapter, the support offered by Turkey and Greece in repelling Iraqi aggression against Kuwait was extremely significant. Furthermore, the experience in conducting joint operations gained by U.S. and European forces in countless NATO exercises was cited by allied military leaders as one of the principal reasons for the smoothness with which Operation Desert Storm was carried out. Had the operation depended on the coordination of Greek and Turkish forces, the results might have been different.

Lack of coordination between Greek and Turkish forces assigned to NATO creates vulnerabilities extending beyond the Aegean that the alliance has sought to disguise rather than eliminate. When NATO was geared exclusively to the containment of the Soviet Union, its military planners did not envisage many tactical situations in wartime in which military forces of the two countries would participate in joint land or maritime operations. The preeminent mission of Greek and Turkish forces was defense of the homeland. In the event of hostilities with the Warsaw Pact, NATO hoped for holding actions in Greek and Turkish Thrace, in the Aegean, and in eastern Turkey that would test Soviet intentions and, in the event of a major Soviet attack, prevent these areas from being overrun before reinforcements arrived from Western Europe and the United States. The coincidence of their national and NATO military missions explains why Greece and Turkey were able to make significant adjustments in their force deployments and defense plans without being directly challenged by NATO's Defense Planning and Military Committees. Although the most casual scrutiny of Greek and Turkish orders of battle clearly showed that their forces in the Aegean theater were deployed primarily against each other, not the Warsaw Pact,[6] NATO chose to treat them as forces executing a national defense mission consistent with NATO plans and not to raise the more awkward question of what threat they were defending themselves against.

NATO commands are essentially planning staffs in peacetime. They do not directly command or control earmarked forces except in NATO exercises of fixed duration whose scenarios, as we have seen, are negotiated in every detail with participating governments. This extremely loose-jointed command structure conforms to the political makeup of a voluntary alliance but encourages NATO's bureaucratic preference for theology over practice, appearance over reality. In the case of Greece and Turkey, it enables the alliance to treat their forces as statistical assets without embroiling NATO in the practical liabilities that made the architects of the alliance hesitant to include them until North Korean forces crossed the 38th Parallel to attack South Korea on June 25, 1950. Even the advisability of inviting Italy to join the organization had been questioned, and it was U.S. pressure (motivated by our dependence on the Azores as a southerly alternative to Shannon and Prestwick for the refueling of piston-driven aircraft on their way to Europe) that proved the determining argument for bringing in Portugal.

The arguments against including Greece and Turkey in the alliance, at a time when both countries were pressing for admission, were summarized in the spring of 1951 by U.S. officials in London in a communication to the permanent under secretary of the British Foreign Office, Lord Strang: The conception of an alliance composed of socially and economically homogeneous countries did not "readily lend itself to the thought of Greek-Turkish participation"; "most parties to the North Atlantic Treaty would probably be reluctant to see a broadening of their security commitments, the immediate benefits of which they [could] not perceive"; and there would be "obvious complications resulting from enlarged membership."[7]

These arguments, which ignored some glaring economic and social disparities among the founding members, would probably have been more influential the year before when the leaders of an untested alliance barely a year old were more concerned with meeting their existing commitments than creating new ones. Greece and Turkey were, after all, even farther from the North Atlantic than Italy. By May 1951, such concerns had been overtaken by events in Korea, and at the next meeting of the North Atlantic Council in Ottawa in September, the members unanimously invited Greece and Turkey to join NATO, with only Norway and the Netherlands expressing any reservations.

At a time when NATO strategists and opinion-leaders in Europe and the United States saw hostilities in Korea as the beginning of a coordinated Soviet campaign of world conquest, perhaps to be followed by renewed military pressure on eastern Turkey and a rekindling of the Greek Civil War, the immediate need to bolster Greece and Turkey far outweighed other considerations.[8] Confronted by what was imagined to be a global Soviet threat, no member of the NATO council, least of all the United States, was disposed to dwell on the longer-term implications of admitting two states with historic bilateral differences and little inclination to resolve them by diplomatic compromise.

When, a month before the Ottawa meeting, the British Embassy in Athens raised with the U.S. ambassador to Greece, John E. Peurifoy, the desirability of warning the Greeks to refrain from stirring up issues (i.e., Cyprus) that might cause difficulties with fellow members (i.e., Britain), Peurifoy, in the words of his reporting cable, "pointed out Dept's reluctance to appear to attach conditions of any kind to Greco-Turk adherence to NATO and presumed this would apply to any formal change of Greek policy re Cyprus."[9]

Having agonized for three years over admitting Greece and Turkey into NATO, the U.S. government, once the decision was made, typically became impatient with modifications. In Washington, more effort is usually required to obtain interagency and congressional support for a new policy than to formulate it or weigh its consequences. The same can be true in obtaining support from allies. As a result, the consensus behind a policy becomes more important than the policy itself, and no one wishes to refine the policy in ways that could threaten the consensus.

In 1948, the NATO Working Group, meeting in Washington to draft the proposed alliance's terms of reference, recognized that if Greece and Turkey were excluded from the pact, some other way of providing for their collective security would have to be found.[10] When, in November 1948, the Turks officially pressed for admission, they were told that while they could not, by definition, be included in a North Atlantic security system, the U.S. and British governments were mindful of their concerns and were studying ways to meet them. The British at first thought that a Mediterranean pact, including Italy as well as Greece and Turkey, might be desirable. It was eventually decided that the U.S. and British governments should issue statements asserting their continued interest in the security of Greece and Turkey. This was done by Secretary of State Dean Acheson and Foreign Secretary Ernest Bevin in statements issued before the North Atlantic Treaty was formally signed on April 4, 1949.

These declarations avoided the danger felt by some founding members of overextending NATO's commitments and permitted the United States and Britain to reaffirm their special security relationship with Greece and Turkey without committing the alliance as a whole. Athens and Ankara, however, were not satisfied with this solution and continued to press for full membership. Had NATO been more conscious of the divisive effects Greek-Turkish differences would have on the alliance's future posture in the eastern Mediterranean and more willing to make full membership contingent on settling them, much of the later trouble might have been avoided. As it was, a climate psychologically favorable to settlement was allowed to dissipate and an opportunity to nudge the parties toward compromise was lost, just as it was lost in different circumstances in the summer of 1974, when the misguided Cyprus policy of the fallen Greek Colonels opened the door to Turkish intervention but also raised the possibility of a negotiated settlement in which the political cost of compromise on the Greek side could have been charged to the account of the Athens junta and not to its elected successors. In the first case, in 1950, reacting to a military crisis outside the area, NATO declined to address the political differences of Greece and Turkey in order to get them into the alliance as quickly as possible. In the second case, in 1974, reacting to a military crisis within the area, NATO declined to address their political differences to avoid driving them out. Even Greece's withdrawal from the allied command structure was not enough to convince NATO, or Washington, that the military price of ignoring political problems in the alliance had become greater than the price of addressing them. NATO scripture supported the view that when members fell out they could take their differences anywhere except the North Atlantic Council.

There is no doubt that NATO's mandate, as conceived by the original signatories, did not include a responsibility for addressing internal disputes. According to Sir Nicholas Henderson, a second secretary of the British Embassy in Washington and a member of the NATO Working Group in 1948, when the French suggested that an "article of conciliation" be introduced into the draft treaty, the other representatives rejected the idea as duplicating existing mechanisms, notably those provided by the United Nations and the International Court of Justice. Henderson comments, "Furthermore, the possibility of disputes between parties to the pact of such serious nature as to defy solution by these existing agencies or under existing treaties seemed to some members of the [Drafting] Committee so remote as to make it unnecessary to establish a further agency of conciliation as between the parties."[11]

The point was underscored later, in 1949, when plenipotentiary representatives of the twelve founding members of NATO agreed that in public statements all signatories would define the primary purpose of the treaty as collective self-defense, under Article 51 of the United Nations Charter, and would not term it a "regional arrangement" under Chapter 8. This was thought to avoid any implication that the North Atlantic treaty aimed at regional conciliation and therefore encroached on UN prerogatives. The parties did, however, affirm their "existing obligations for the maintenance of peace and the settlement of disputes between them."[12]

NATO leaders have not always adhered in practice to the conservative interpretation of the treaty and protocols favored by the original signatories. In the period 1957–1958, two NATO secretaries general, Lord Ismay and Paul-Henri Spaak, acted as mediators in attempts to restore harmony to Anglo-Greek-Turkish relations at a time of mounting violence in Cyprus and successive confrontations between Greece and Turkey. Unsuccessful though they were in producing a settlement, these efforts did bring about a resumption of talks between Athens and Ankara that eventually made possible the Zurich and London accords of 1959–1960 by which Cyprus gained its independence. The United States took no part in NATO's diplomatic initiatives but President Dwight D. Eisenhower expressed public support for Lord Ismay's role in 1957.

In 1964, the United States endorsed an even bolder NATO intervention in the Cyprus problem. As we saw in chapter 2, violence between Greek and Turkish Cypriots had again broken out at the end of 1963; the Turks were poised to intervene militarily; and the British were seeking to prevent the total collapse of the Zurich and London accords, of which they, the Greeks, and the Turks were guarantors. The British proposal was to establish an international peacekeeping force on Cyprus composed of contingents drawn exclusively from NATO countries. After an initially negative reaction, the United States not only agreed to support this British proposal but to contribute a U.S. force of 1,200 men.[13] Anglo-American efforts to place a NATO peacekeeping force on Cyprus were soon abandoned, however, when President Makarios, sensitive to anything that could jeopardize the nonaligned status of Cyprus, categorically rejected the idea.

Instead, the United Nations peacekeeping force that is still in Cyprus emerged from the 1964 crisis. Indeed, aside from diplomatic démarches made in 1967 by Secretary General Manlio Brosio in support of the Vance mission,[14] no NATO role in resolving the political differences between Greece and Turkey in

Cyprus or the Aegean has been seriously contemplated since that time. This was due to practical considerations, not a stricter reading of the NATO treaty and protocols.

It is assumed by many NATO officials, and has become conventional wisdom for their national governments, that any undertaking to resolve Greek-Turkish differences is a no-win proposition for the alliance, which already has as much as it can handle keeping Western Europe, Canada, and the United States marching in step without also trying to bring harmony to the southeastern flank, whose members are considered to be less schooled in team play. If NATO proves its impartiality by maintaining an attitude of detached concern, it is sometimes argued, Athens and Ankara will eventually realize that the alliance is not going to bail them out. Only then will they accept the responsibility for resolving their own differences.

This reasoning ignores the fact that neither Greece nor Turkey presently believes that NATO *is* impartial. Each is convinced that the alliance tilts in favor of the other. The Greeks believe that strategic considerations—the notorious realpolitik— invariably give Turkey more weight in NATO councils because of its larger population and troop strength, its 380-mile land border with the Soviet Union, and its control of the Dardanelles. The Turks, on the other hand, believe that the true significance of their membership is qualified by its purely strategic character. Whenever Turkish and Greek interests collide, they contend, NATO is inclined to support Greece with which Europe and the United States have stronger historical and cultural affinities. Greeks and Turks both, in other words, consider that NATO undervalues their membership, albeit for different reasons.

Paradoxically, the alliance's present hands-off policy, although intended to project NATO's impartiality and encourage Athens and Ankara to settle their own differences, seems to be having the opposite effect. Both capitals are led to interpret NATO's attitude as proof that the organization does not take them seriously and, accordingly, to see less prospect for rewards from the alliance, should they adopt more flexible policies, or penalties, should they fail to do so. It is also logical to suppose that what Greeks and Turks alike view as the relatively low priority accorded to the southeastern flank gives them little reason to place NATO priorities above their own when it comes to force planning and deployment, weapons procurement, and other aspects of their national defense policy. If this reasoning is correct, a less perfunctory reaction to the Greek-Turkish dispute and more vigorous diplomacy on the part of the alliance would not only put NATO in the position of addressing a problem it has too long neglected but might elicit a more serious effort at conflict resolution from the Greeks and Turks. But inducing the alliance to bestir itself diplomatically will require, first of all, a more active U.S. interest.

From the standpoint of the United States, sponsorship of Greek and Turkish membership in NATO was really a way of institutionalizing and, at the same time, sharing the responsibility to implement the commitment to defend them undertaken through the Truman Doctrine. For their part, Greece and Turkey initially regarded their NATO membership as essentially a reinforcement of earlier U.S. guarantees.

Since 1952, the perceived significance of the NATO link has changed appreciably in both countries. Greece came to regard its NATO membership as a buffer, not primarily against the Warsaw Pact, but against Turkey, and as a reinforcement of its ties, not to the United States, but to Europe. Indeed, one of the significant benefits of NATO membership to the Greek government is that it "Europeanizes" to some extent the small but controversial U.S. military presence in Greece. While NATO has not won any popularity contests in Greece since 1974, Greek public opinion polls consistently show a majority in favor of continued membership, in part to counterbalance Turkish influence in NATO, and in part because NATO security programs are less suspect than those conducted in Greece by the United States, whose defense policies are believed by many Greeks to be unduly influenced by Turkish demands and by domestic Greek political considerations, namely, by a perceived U.S. desire to strengthen Greek conservatives at the expense of the Greek left. Thus, when the Greek and U.S. governments have engaged in negotiations on shared military facilities in Greece, it has usually been easier to agree on their NATO than their bilateral roles, even when, as we saw in chapter 1, no public reference to NATO appears, as in the text of the 1983 Defense and Economic Cooperation Agreement.

Turkey has also come to look on NATO to some extent as a safeguard against over-reliance on the United States, specifically against the uncertainties of doing business with the U.S. government, whose security policies are thought to be unduly influenced by Greece—or at least by partisans of Greece in Congress—and by domestic political considerations, namely by the perceived political weight of the "Greek lobby." During the period of the U.S. arms embargo, between 1975 and 1978, Turkey relied heavily on the continuing flow of military assistance from another NATO partner, the Federal Republic of Germany, to compensate for the interruption of supplies from the United States.

Even under the new conditions prevailing in the aftermath of the Cold War NATO has, therefore, certain assets if it decides to play a more active diplomatic role in the southeastern sector. It can offer its good offices to Greece and Turkey with the assurance that extraneous political influences—deemed unavoidable when the United States involves itself directly in Greek-Turkish problems—will be minimized and that whatever settlement is reached will be backed by a group of states allied militarily to both Greece and Turkey but with varying degrees of intimacy based on political complexion, historic links, and the chemistry of their leaders. Either as a mediator or friendly advisor, NATO could employ a combination of flexibility and leverage unavailable to any single member, including the United States.

Andrew Wilson, in his 1979 monograph, *The Aegean Dispute,* a meticulous and dispassionate analysis of Aegean problems and Cyprus, concludes, "The more one studies the [Greek-Turkish] dispute and talks with those involved, the more one realizes that what is often largely at issue, apart from lack of confidence, is national pride." [15]

Anyone who has had occasion to discuss these matters with individual Greeks or Turks will agree. It is for this very reason that a third-party role is essential. When national pride interprets flexibility as weakness and tradeoffs as capitulations, a third party can sometimes assume enough of the political risk to enable the disputants to reach a settlement that serves their longer-term interests. In assuming the risk itself, the third party may of course endanger its own interests by alienating one or both of the parties directly involved. This is why NATO has been so reticent about Greek-Turkish differences in recent years. But there are also risks in reticence, and one of them is that an inherently unstable status quo will explode into violence that no one wants but no one has done much to prevent.

If the element of national pride is put aside, and with it the heightened sensitivity to political risk that national pride entails, it is clear that the present state of Greek-Turkish relations works against everyone's interests. The Cyprus problem costs Athens and Ankara resources they can ill afford to expend, needlessly engages their national prestige in an area that neither controls, and makes it infinitely harder for them to resolve their differences in the areas they do control. The petroleum resources, if any, of the Aegean shelf remain unexplored and unexploited by either party. Territorial sea and air spaces have become weak points to be defended rather than strong points in the common defense. The Athens FIR loses operational effectiveness as an air traffic control center to the extent that Greece tries to invest it with political authority that Turkey disputes. Aegean command-and-control lines, which assure interlocking defenses when they are compatible, have produced military gridlock ever since they became a matter of dispute in 1974.

Neither side, in other words, benefits from a situation in which all of its longer-term political, economic, and military interests are subordinated to inconclusive tests of national sovereignty. Because national pride is often a poor guide to national interest, the undoing of much that has been done in the name of national defense would actually strengthen the security of both countries. It would unquestionably also strengthen the security of NATO, which no longer faces a clearly defined external threat but would be prudent to strengthen its internal unity against an uncertain future characterized by turbulent instability in Eastern Europe and the Middle East, two areas whose strategic

importance to Western Europe and the United States is impossible to ignore.

If these desirable things are to happen, however, Greece and
Turkey will have to be convinced that the potential diplomatic
and economic advantages of compromise outweigh the domestic
political risks and that, in the 1990s, they, like France and Germany 30 years earlier, are capable of transcending their history
and constructing a new and more forward-looking relationship.

6

WHEN GREEK MEETS TURK

The relationship of France and Germany until their reconciliation in 1963 bears more than a passing resemblance to that of Greece and Turkey today. Even their national personalities contrast in similar ways. Greeks, with their passion for political thrust-and-parry, their fascination with conspiracies and conspiracy theories, their impatience, and the cynicism they feel toward their leaders, are probably closer in temperament to the French than to any other nationality. Turks—patient, pragmatic, hierarchical, and rigorous—seem closer in spirit to the Germans, with whom they also share an instinct for realpolitik and a dogged consistency in their pursuit of national objectives. The stereotypical images that Greeks and Turks have of each other—particularly apparent in the press and schoolbooks of each country—are distorted projections of these characteristics. The Greek becomes guileful, mendacious, and unreliable; the Turk ruthless, brutal, and aggressive. This, too, has its counterpart in Franco-German relations.

Having said this, it must be added that Greece and Turkey have historically interacted very differently than France and Germany. There is no counterpart in Franco-German history to the four centuries of Ottoman Turkish suzerainty over the Greeks—a period in which many talented Greeks were either encadred in the services of the sultan or, if they had the means to do so, went into exile. Those who lacked the means to escape or the willingness to be assimilated remained as a Greek "nation" (or *millet,* as the Turks referred to communities of subject minorities), separate from the Turkish population but in close proximity to it. This pattern of demographic dispersal helps explain why there is today much more evidence of cultural familiarity between Greeks and Turks at the popular level than among the educated elites. This is certainly untrue of France and Germany, where the popular cultures are distinctive but the interchange among the elites has been almost continuous for the past 200 years. This difference may also explain why Greece and Turkey have been less successful in achieving political reconciliation than France and Germany and why they will need more help from outside if they are to succeed.

Needless to say, these comparisons cannot be pushed too far—Greeks and Turks are very much the products of their own historical experience—but a diplomat dealing with these countries, or encouraging their leaders to deal more flexibly with each other, will do well to be aware of them, as he will to be aware of a trait that Greeks and Turks have in common: strong national pride and a propensity to see disagreements as challenges or affronts to it. Greece and Turkey, no less than France and Germany—and with more historical justification—are acutely conscious that they represent different cultures and civilizations. If they were not, their contemporary differences would have been resolved long ago.

Feuds between nations, like feuds between clans, usually arise from disputes over property that are aggravated by proximity and sustained by just enough cultural familiarity to breed contempt. The engagements of great national rivals can be as sanguinary as those of civil wars and yet, like the battlefields of civil wars, delineate common ground. For Greece and Turkey this is true in a literal sense. The ground they fought on is the ground they fought over.

As incompatible as the religions, value systems, and national personalities of the Greeks and Turks are, their long struggle has been over territory—first the grudging retreat of the Byzantine Greeks from what is now Anatolian Turkey, Istanbul, and Turkish Thrace, then the slow, serial withdrawal of the Ottoman Turks from what is now mainland Greece, Cyprus, and the Greek archipelago. Religious and ethnic singularities complicate the Greek-Turkish rivalry, and differing national personalities give it an abrasive edge, but the essence of the dispute is still territorial.

This is no longer true, however, in an irredentist sense. Neither Greece nor Turkey has outstanding legal claims against the territory of the other[1] or is even seeking border rectifications.

Issues of sovereignty abound, but these arise from differing interpretations of international agreements or conventions that affect the way sovereignty can be exercised in specific areas. Sovereignty itself is not being challenged. Even in the case of Cyprus, where Turkish troops remain almost two decades after the amphibious operation that brought them there in the summer of 1974, the underlying diplomatic problem is to define how, if at all, Cypriot sovereignty was qualified by the 1959 Zurich and London accords making Cyprus independent. Ankara argues that its military intervention was justified under the treaty of guarantee embodied in the accords and that it had no other means of protecting the Turkish Cypriot minority after the Athens junta violated the accords by engineering a coup against the legitimate government of Cyprus. The treaty of guarantee calls for consultation among the three guarantor powers—Greece, Turkey, and the United Kingdom—adding that, if concerted action proves impossible, " . . . each of the three guaranteeing powers reserves the right to take action with the sole aim of re-establishing the state of affairs created by the present treaty."[2] That the guarantors could reserve the right to intervene militarily in the affairs of Cyprus is hotly disputed by Athens and Nicosia,[3] who argue that no "right" can be superior to the pledge undertaken by member states of the United Nations to "refrain . . . from the threat or use of force against the territorial integrity or political independence of any state. . . . "[4]

But the Turkish legal position, whether one accepts it or not, has some positive implications. It implies that Turkey accepts as legitimate the goal of "re-establishing the state of affairs created by the present treaty," that is, it accepts the concept of a single sovereign state of Cyprus, and it implies that Ankara's support for the "Turkish Republic of Northern Cyprus," whose independence Turkey alone recognizes, is negotiable. Even the Cyprus problem, in other words, which has touched off the most frequent and violent Greek-Turkish clashes since World War II, is what lawyers call a *casus foederis,* a case covered by treaty, which is to say that it has the prerequisites for a negotiated settlement based on the sovereignty of a single Cyprus state, adequate safeguards for the ethnic communities, and the withdrawal of Turkish troops.

Where legal disputes exist, so do legal remedies. The encouraging aspect of the Greek-Turkish confrontation, whether in Cyprus or the Aegean, is that its political, economic, and military components will become negotiable if its non-negotiable component, their intense mutual distrust, can be mitigated. This has happened in the past, usually as the aftermath of a head-on collision, such as the Asia Minor debacle of 1922 when Greece, with the encouragement of its World War I allies, especially the British, attempted the military occupation of southwestern Turkey and was disastrously routed by the Turks under the command of Mustapha Kemal, soon to become the first president of the new Turkish republic. Out of these traumatic events came the Lausanne Treaty of 1923 involving a massive exchange of populations that left residual minorities of only 110,000 Orthodox Christians in Turkey, most of them ethnically Greek, and about 120,000 Moslems in Greek Thrace, most of them ethnically Turkish. Something similar happened when the Zurich and London accords eventually emerged from the wreckage of the Istanbul riots of September 1955 and the escalating campaign of violence undertaken by EOKA in Cyprus. Even the détente in Greek-Turkish relations achieved by prime ministers Andreas Papandreou and Turgut Özal in the first half of 1988 was a reaction to a dispute about oil prospecting on the Aegean shelf in March of the previous year that brought the two countries again to the brink of war.

The Cyprus crisis of 1974, on the other hand, violent though it was, generated little diplomatic momentum when the bloodshed ended. This is almost certainly because the newly formed Karamanlis government in Athens decided to avoid a military clash with Turkey. Most Greeks today believe that the decision was justified, given the preceding seven years of military and political mismanagement by the Athens junta, but it left in them a sense of bitter frustration that complicates the search for negotiated solutions to all their problems with Turkey.

In this century Greece and Turkey have experienced two periods of rapprochement. One occurred between 1945 and

1955 and, as we have seen, was induced by their common sense of insecurity in the face of a perceived Soviet threat. The other occurred between 1930 and 1940 but was neither the response to an outside threat nor to an immediately preceding disaster. It deserves attention for this reason and also because its architects were two of the strongest nationalists to lead Greece and Turkey in modern times, Eleftherios Venizelos and Kemal Ataturk. It was to this bold but transient peace initiative that Secretary Dulles referred in his ill-advised parallel letters to Athens and Ankara in 1955.

Although the Lausanne Treaty had dealt with some of the most contentious of the problems facing Greece and Turkey after World War I, all of which had been brought to a head by Greece's Anatolian adventure, a great many issues remained unresolved. The Greeks sought financial compensation for property abandoned by 1,500,000 refugees who had either fled Turkey or been involved in the formal exchange of populations negotiated at Lausanne. They also wanted explicit Turkish assurances that Ankara had no claims against Greek territory. The Turks were reluctant to pay financial compensation in the amounts being claimed by Greece, but—with memories of the Greek military campaign in Asia Minor still fresh—they also wanted a renewed Greek pledge not to seek changes in the boundaries drawn at Lausanne. As recounted by one recent Greek author, during the period 1924–1926, Turkey

> had sought, in parallel with . . . the resolution of economic questions, the signature of a treaty of friendship, something rejected by the Greek government which maintained that conclusion of such an agreement would have no practical effect if economic subjects remained pending. . . . In the negotiations which began at the end of 1927, Greece proposed the resolution of all differences by means of arbitration. The Turkish Government persistently rejected this solution, without however ceasing to declare the need for understanding.[5]

By 1928, negotiations had proceeded far enough for the Turkish foreign minister to tell the *Journal de Gèneve* in March that Turkey no longer had anything to fear from Greece and, in fact, favored a stronger Greece as a "source of protection for Turkey."[6] In July of the same year, Venizelos stated his belief that Turkey "has no designs on our territory and . . . can be certain that we have no designs whatsoever on theirs."[7] By the end of August 1930, Venizelos was ready to convey to Ankara a proposal for a treaty of friendship, nonaggression, and arbitration. It appears that although the resolution of economic differences was still extremely important to the Greek side, "for Venizelos preeminent significance was accorded to eliciting a public acknowledgement from Turkey that it accepted the territorial status quo [*kathestos*] as defined by existing agreements."[8] The willingness of Venizelos to subordinate Greece's financial claims to the territorial issue was criticized heatedly by refugee leaders; but on October 30, 1930, the Treaty of Friendship, Neutrality and Arbitration was signed in Ankara in the course of Venizelos's historic visit to the Turkish capital.

It is apparent from an examination of the diplomatic prelude to the 1930 treaty that even the strong leadership of Venizelos and Ataturk might not have been sufficient to bring it into being had a third party not involved itself dynamically in the process. In the late 1920s, Mussolini's Italy hoped to expand its influence in the eastern Mediterranean. Mussolini himself considered the conclusion of treaties of friendship by Italy with Greece and Turkey to be important steps in this direction, particularly if the Italians were then able to persuade Athens and Ankara to resolve their differences and conclude a similar treaty with each other. In a telegram to the Italian ambassador in Athens in May 1928, Mussolini expressed confidence that the Greek government would agree to sign a pact with Italy on the formal assurance that Mussolini would personally exert pressure on the Turks to show greater flexibility toward Greece.[9] Once treaties of friendship with both Turkey and Greece had been concluded, Mussolini told his ambassador, a third treaty, this time between Greece and Turkey, would be the "crowning achievement" of Italian diplomacy. In the event, the Greeks were extremely hesitant about signing a pact with Italy before Mussolini had redeemed his promise to apply leverage on Turkey. At the time, Venizelos was conducting a complex diplomatic strategy of his own, the object of which was to strengthen Greek security through a series of bilateral agreements, each of which would lead into and reinforce the others. Thus, Greece signed its treaty with Italy in September 1928, reached a similar accord with Yugoslavia in 1929, and finally signed the treaty with Turkey in 1930. The diplomatic record seems to bear out Iphigenia Anastasiadou's judgment that the Italian role in negotiation of the Venizelos-Ataturk treaty was "decisive if not determining." [10]

From a review of this episode several points emerge that are relevant to the situation today. First, the outstanding issues between Greece and Turkey after the 1923 Lausanne settlement were the question of financial compensation for the Greek refugees from Asia Minor and the question of territorial security. By compromising on the issue of financial compensation, Greece and Turkey—especially the former, since Venizelos, at some political cost to himself, accepted a Turkish offer of compensation far below the amount sought by the refugees—demonstrated that the fundamental objective of the 1930 treaty of friendship was to allay concerns about territorial security. Second, to conclude the treaty on less than optimum terms, the presence of strong, nationalist leaders was an advantage, not an impediment—again, especially in Greece's case. Third, the assistance of a third party, Italy, was essential in bringing Greeks and Turks together. It is also worth noting that over half a century ago the Turks were no more interested in the international arbitration of financial differences than they are now in taking the Aegean shelf controversy to the International Court of Justice, and that the Greeks initially attached a higher priority, as they do now, to the resolution of specific issues—in 1928, financial compensation for the refugees, and today, the withdrawal of Turkish troops from Cyprus—than to the conclusion of a general treaty of friendship and nonaggression. In 1930, the willingness of both sides to soften their positions on the financial question was expressed only after they had satisfied each other that territorial claims were being set aside.

The détente in Greek-Turkish relations that began with the 1930 treaty lasted about ten years, until the Italo-German attack on Greece in 1940–1941, when Turkish neutrality was interpreted as an unfriendly attitude by the Greeks, who contended that Ankara had an obligation to come to their aid under the 1939 treaties of mutual assistance that Turkey had signed with

Britain and France. The Greek reaction to Turkey's 1941 nonaggression pact with Bulgaria was even stronger. Nevertheless, the 1930 treaty of friendship had already produced advances in Greek-Turkish relations, vindicating the belief of Venizelos and Ataturk that both countries would benefit from friendly relations and secure frontiers.

In late 1930 or early 1931, Venizelos, in a move not often recalled in recent times by Greeks or Turks, actually nominated Ataturk for the Nobel Peace Prize, citing his successful consolidation of the new Turkish republic and his policy of "peace at home, peace abroad." At the same time, Venizelos shrewdly used his nominating letter to the Nobel Committee as a means of reinforcing Ataturk's commitment on the territorial issue.[11] His letter, undated copies of which repose in the Venizelos Archives in Athens, informs the committee that "in actuality, Turkey did not hesitate to accept honorably the loss of territories settled by other nationalities and, [now] frankly satisfied with the ethnic and political boundaries that have been defined by treaty, has become a mainstay of peace in the Near East." The Nobel Committee did not act favorably on Ataturk's nomination but not for lack of effort by Venizelos, who tirelessly promoted Greek-Turkish fraternity until his death in 1936.

Venizelos not only praised the good-neighbor policies of the Turkish republic under Ataturk but joined with the Turkish leader in arguing that Greeks and Turks shared a common Aryan descent. On one occasion, writing in the weekly newspaper, *Ergasia,* he asked rhetorically: "How many Turks are calculated to have come to Asia Minor from central Asia?" and answered, "Probably a few hundred thousands, who multiplied twenty, thirty or forty times in the Hellenized lands of Asia Minor and Pontos, which constituted for centuries the backbone of the Byzantine Empire, and of which (by the time Constantinople fell to the Ottomans) a large part had already been Turkified."[12]

This argument for Greek-Turkish consanguinity has made few converts among ethnologists, and the relatively late migration of the Turks from central Asia to Hellenic Asia Minor[13] is reflected in differences of religion, language, and custom that run counter to theories of a common descent. It is undeniable, however, that 400 years of Ottoman rule over Greek lands and people produced extensive cultural imbrication—in folklore, vernacular speech, music, and cuisine—that represents a solid, if seldom avowed, foundation for popular rapport when political discord has been composed. The Greek Orthodox church itself faces in two directions, like the Byzantine double-headed eagle, since, in its extreme doctrinal conservatism Greek Orthodoxy views the Latin church with as much distrust as Islam. The Frankish occupation in the thirteenth century of most of what constitutes modern Greece, which was the outcome of the errant Fourth Crusade, left wounds as deep as those later inflicted by the Ottomans. Patrick Leigh Fermor observes that both Greek and Turkish villagers sometimes refer to western Europeans as "Franks" who inhabit either "Frankia" (in Greek) or "Frangistan" (in Turkish).[14]

Greeks and Turks have, in fact, managed to coexist peacefully at the local level through long periods of their history—in Asia Minor, in Thrace, and in Cyprus. When violence has erupted, it has more often than not been the result of disputes among their leaders. Under the Ottoman *millet* system, the Greek Orthodox subjects of the sultan enjoyed extensive powers of self-government and a privileged position among minorities. It was only as the Ottoman Empire lapsed into decadence and the Greek leadership initiated the struggle for national independence in the early 1800s that violence became widespread at the community level. Later still, in Cyprus, the Greek and Turkish Cypriot populations lived peacefully enough side by side, often intermingled in the same villages, until, in the 1950s, the Greek drive for *enosis* and the retaliatory Turkish demand for partition brought them into open conflict.[15]

The coexistence of Greeks and Turks in the same areas over long periods of time, contrary to the theorizing of Venizelos, has not produced genuine assimilation on a wide basis. As a matter of fact, it has been by preserving their differences that the Greeks and Turks have managed to live side by side peacefully when political strife was not driving them apart. It is precisely because the Moslem population of Greek Thrace is so clearly distinguishable that, however controversial its status may become at times of tension between Greece and Turkey, the "Moslem question" in western Thrace will always be more manageable and less potentially disruptive than the "Macedonian question." The latter involves the interests of three states—Greece, Bulgaria, and Yugoslavia—not two, and is rendered almost insoluble by lack of agreement on who the Macedonians actually are.[16]

This is not to say that the grievances of the remaining Greek Orthodox in Turkey and of the Turkish Moslems living in Greece cannot and do not aggravate relations between Athens and Ankara. They do. In February 1990, the Turkish consul general in the northern Greek town of Komotini was declared persona non grata by the Greek government on charges that he had referred to local Moslems as "fellow countrymen." In reprisal, the Turks demanded the recall of the Greek consul general in Istanbul. This diplomatic incident followed demonstrations and clashes between Orthodox and Moslem residents of Komotini sparked by the parliamentary election campaign then taking place and accusations in the Greek press that the Turkish government was interfering in the internal affairs of Greece under cover of its consular operations. Turkish state radio was likewise charged with interference in the elections through its broadcasts to Greece. Turkey denied these charges and went on to enumerate a number of issues—expropriation of Moslem property by Greek authorities, inadequate provision for education in the Turkish language, and obstacles imposed on the awarding of licenses for vehicles, like tractors, essential to farming—that Ankara contends reveal discrimination by Greece against its Moslem minority.

Athens, while rejecting these charges, points out that whereas the community of 120,000 Moslems who remained in Greek Thrace after the 1923 exchange of populations has grown to an estimated 130,000, in Turkey the 1923 Orthodox community of 110,000 has been reduced today to about 5,000. There are reasons for the disparity that numbers alone do not explain. The Greek Orthodox minority in Turkey was in general more affluent, less tied to the land, and therefore more mobile than the Moslem minority in Greece, most of whom were in 1923, and are today, farmers. In addition, the higher birth rate of the Moslem population suggests that many may have migrated to Turkey without significantly reducing the total number of those who have chosen to remain in western Thrace. Nevertheless, violent and highly visible Turkish eruptions of anti-Greek sentiment, like the 1955 Istanbul riots, are easier to document than the kinds of bureaucratic discrimination that seem to characterize Greek behavior and have unquestionably been more destructive to Greek-Turkish relations.

It would be profitless here to attempt a detailed analysis of the minorities question or to make a judgment about where the ultimate responsibility for discrimination and, when it occurs, violence really lies. We know from the record of the Turkish trials of the leaders of the Menderes government that Turkish political leaders were implicated in the 1955 riots in Istanbul. We also know from official Greek revelations that General Grivas, with the connivance of the Athens junta, touched off the Cyprus crisis of 1974. Beyond these episodes, in which the hand of the political leadership in Ankara and Athens is clearly discernible, we can only observe that the historical evidence suggests that Greeks and Turks can live together peaceably, while remaining loyal to their own customs and cultures, when the political climate cultivated by their leaders permits them to do so.[17]

If today's Greek and Turkish political leaders, manifestly less able than Ataturk and Venizelos to free themselves from the constraints of history, are to cultivate a better climate of relations, they will need help in addressing the fundamental issues in dispute, starting with the issue that was the key to progress in 1930 and remains so today—territorial security. This is where the United States and NATO seem the logical parties to play a more active and constructive political role than they have in the past. How they might do so we will explore more carefully in the next chapter.

7

STEPS TOWARD A SOLUTION: THE TERRITORIAL ISSUE

There is abundant evidence to show that the Greek and Turkish governments, although themselves disavowing irredentism, believe that concealed territorial ambitions lie at the core of each other's bilateral and multilateral differences. Thus, in the mid-1980s, both governments published glossy brochures, with colored photographs and maps, to set forth their respective positions on the various Aegean issues. The English-language edition of the Greek brochure, titled, *Threat in the Aegean,* after quoting a series of statements by Turkish officials questioning the "Greekness" of the Aegean Sea and the legal status of the Greek Aegean islands, states its view of Turkish objectives in these words:

> Turkey aspires towards a partition of the Aegean airspace and finally towards partition of the entire Aegean sea area and consequently to isolate the eastern Aegean islands and to erode their legal status—something which eventually will provide Turkey with sufficient grounds to accommodate its expansionist goals.[1]

The Turkish brochure, published as a response to the Greek presentation in a virtually identical format under the title, *The Aegean Realities,* also carries quotations, attributed in this case to Greek political and ecclesiastical leaders who seem to be suggesting that the *megali idea*—the historical concept of a greater Greek state embracing Istanbul, southwestern Anatolia, and Cyprus—remains the ultimate goal of Greek foreign policy. According to the Turkish brochure:

> In essence, all the issues that Turkey faces today in her relations with Greece are reflections of the same Greek ambition to expand towards the east at the expense of Turkey.[2]

Territorial security is therefore the issue that both governments emphasize in their official propaganda, and after discounting the hyperbole that characterizes any war of words, we can infer that concern about territorial security is still, as it was in 1930, fundamental to their suspicions and antagonism, beclouding their other differences and impairing their vision of how to resolve them. But if the two governments were capable of laying the territorial issue to rest before, why do they find it so difficult to do so now? The blood that has been shed in Cyprus since 1974 is certainly a powerful disincentive. It is not, however, a more intractable obstacle to détente than the barriers overcome by Ataturk and Venizelos 60 years ago.

There are, to be sure, differences in the relative strengths and power positions of Greece and Turkey that have developed in the past half century that affect their leaders' approach to questions of national security. Greece in 1930, although it had been defeated by the Turks in Asia Minor eight years earlier, remained an important factor in Balkan and eastern Mediterranean affairs and still benefited from the support of powerful allies, notably Britain. (Venizelos, in particular, had earned British gratitude by bringing Greece into World War I on the side of the Entente powers.) Turkey, on the other hand, was mainly preoccupied by internal developments in 1930, as Ataturk sought to create a new secular republic out of the ruins of the Ottoman Empire. Moreover, Turkey had been on the losing side in World War I and still felt itself isolated from both Europe and the Middle East. It was only in 1932 that the Turkish republic joined the League of Nations. Turkey's relative isolation in the 1920s, partly the result of the Ottoman collapse and partly of Kemalist isolationism, had the effect of reducing Turkey's weight in international affairs and, more specifically, the leverage Ankara could apply to Athens in settling bilateral disputes.

Turkey today, despite persistent economic problems and a per capita GNP that is one of the lowest in Europe,[3] is a much stronger power than it was in 1930, both militarily and diplomatically. Its population, growing at the rate of 2.5 percent a year, is now about five times that of Greece, which has a population growth rate near zero; its military strength is proportionately greater than Greece's, in numbers if not in training or readiness; and as a member of NATO in good standing it is no longer diplomatically isolated, as it was in 1930.

Greece, on the other hand, while it returned to the military structure of NATO in 1980 and has avoided the worst of Turkey's economic problems, like an inflation rate of 50 percent or more annually, has, by its withdrawal from NATO commands in 1974 and its dissociation from many alliance policies during the years of the Papandreou government, tended to isolate itself from other members. Since 1974, successive Greek governments have been less skillful than their Turkish counterparts in protecting national interests without appearing to do so at the expense of the alliance as a whole. Episodes like the Turkish government's refusal, in April 1989, to permit U.S. inspection of a MIG-29 flown to Turkey by a defecting Soviet pilot, are reminders that Ankara's priorities are not always those of NATO. Nevertheless, the Turks, by effective diplomacy and with a more consistent view of their strategic priorities, have, unlike the Greeks, successfully cultivated an impression in NATO councils that they wish to minimize the distracting impact of bilateral controversies upon the alliance.

Given this assessment of the altered power positions of Greece and Turkey since 1930, it is easy to see why Athens feels insecure in its confrontation with Ankara. Turkey is not only larger than Greece but has received at least 30 percent more military equipment than Greece over the past 40 years, most of it from the United States. In the event of hostilities, whether in Cyprus or the Aegean, logistics, as much as raw manpower, would favor Turkey. Why, in these circumstances, would Turkey be interested in territorial guarantees?

Three reasons come to mind. First, although an element of uncertainty in Greece's ability to protect its islands off the Anatolian coast may serve Turkish interests, the same cannot be said of the buffer zone in Cyprus lightly patrolled by the UN Force in Cyprus,[4] which separates Turkish-controlled northern Cyprus from the rest of the island. Here, although logistic factors are even more favorable to the Turkish side than in the Aegean, a serious breach in peacekeeping arrangements would create enormous problems for Turkey, diplomatic as much as military. In another round of fighting in Cyprus, Ankara would not be protecting only an ethnic Turkish minority. It would be allying itself with the self-proclaimed Turkish Republic of Northern Cyprus against the universally recognized Republic of Cyprus, a member of the United Nations and an active participant in the councils of the nonaligned. Whatever the course of military developments might be—and Turkish Cypriots would be outnumbered four or five to one—the effect on Turkey's international position, including its position in NATO, would be catastrophic. Ankara therefore would greatly benefit from stabilizing the status quo until a negotiated settlement of the Cyprus problem, including the withdrawal of Turkish troops from the northern sector, was achieved.

Second, whether the Turkish Fourth (or Aegean) Army numbers 30,000 troops, as the Turks claim, or 150,000, as the Greeks claim, whether it is a training command, as Ankara insists, or an amphibious assault force, as Athens says, these are forces deployed in the wrong place at the wrong time from Turkey's standpoint. They are certainly not needed to defend Turkey from a possible military thrust from the Greek islands, which would be suicidal for the Greeks to contemplate. Given the volatile situation along Turkey's southern border with Syria and Iraq, Ankara would be able to employ the men of the Fourth Army more effectively in these sectors if the political need to base them opposite the Greek islands of the Aegean were removed. The Persian Gulf crisis that erupted in August 1990, in which Ankara aligned itself against Baghdad, shutting down the flow of Iraqi oil conveyed by pipeline across southern Turkey to the Mediterranean, showed clearly where Turkey's strategic interests lie in the foreseeable future. Press reports indicate that by the end of 1990 Turkey had reinforced its forces along the Iraqi frontier with 100,000 men.

The final reason for Turkey to be interested in territorial guarantees is that, by declining to enter into formal undertakings not to alter existing territorial arrangements by force, Ankara would be preserving a military threat it almost certainly has no intention of carrying out at the expense of a legal and diplomatic position that it needs to shore up. Turkey may no longer be isolated in world affairs, but as long as Turkish troops remain in Cyprus, it is often on the defensive—in the United Nations, the

Conference on Security and Cooperation in Europe (CSCE), the U.S. Congress, and even in NATO. To the extent that Turkey's military strength is perceived to be directed against Greece and Cyprus, it becomes a political weakness. Given Turkey's need for economic assistance from western Europe and the United States, and the high priority it assigns to gaining admission to the European Community, putting to rest Greek uncertainties on the territorial issue would cost Turkey little but offer the prospect of substantial benefits in the future.

These must have been some of the factors that President Özal had in mind in the spring of 1989 when, speaking as prime minister, he told an interviewer from the Greek periodical *Agora* that he was "open to the signing of a non-aggression pact after the Greek elections."[5] The Greek elections that took place in June 1989, immediately after Özal's interview, produced a provisional coalition government composed of conservatives and Communists, whose limited mandate did not include major foreign policy initiatives. However, the conservative government elected ten months later, on April 8, 1990, under Prime Minister Constantine Mitsotakis, has the authority to negotiate a nonaggression pact with Turkey if it chooses to do so.

The official Greek position, as we have seen, calls for the withdrawal of Turkish troops from Cyprus before negotiating other differences with Turkey. This was the position of the Papandreou government, and it has been reaffirmed by Mitsotakis. At the same time, successive Greek governments have shown their territorial insecurity by seeking guarantees in various forms from the United States against any attempt to settle Greek-Turkish differences by other than peaceful means. The United States, although reluctant to be drawn into the dispute between its two allies, provided reassuring language to the Greeks in 1976, as we have seen, in the form of the Kissinger-Bitsios letter.[6] Later, the preamble to the U.S.-Greek Mutual Defense Cooperation Agreement (DCA) signed in Athens on May 30, 1990, renewed these assurances. In this agreement, the two parties declare "their commitment to respect the principle of refraining from actions threatening to peace" and reiterate "their firm determination mutually to safeguard and protect the

sovereignty, independence and territorial integrity of their respective countries against actions threatening to peace, including
armed attack or threat thereof; and confirm their resolve to
oppose actively and unequivocally any such attempt or action
and their commitment to make appropriate major efforts to
prevent such a course of action." Later in the preamble, the
United States and Greece "reaffirm their dedication to the principle that international disputes shall be settled through peaceful
means; and their continuing firm resolve to contribute actively to
the early and just settlement of existing international disputes in
the region which particularly concern either party to this agreement. . . . "[7]

The Turkish government's reaction to the wording of the
preamble was extremely hostile. After showing its displeasure by
limiting Turkish attendance at the U.S. ambassador's Fourth of
July reception in 1990, Ankara extracted from Washington various public disclaimers that the preamble was directed against
Turkey. When the process of "clarification" had been completed,
the only thing that was clear was that another well-intentioned
U.S. initiative had gone awry, leaving the Turks and Greeks
confused about U.S. policy but with new grounds for distrusting
each other.[8]

Greece's search for reassurance has also led it to appeal to
NATO for guarantees. Starting in 1981, the Papandreou government preferred (for its own domestic political reasons) not to
appear to be supplicating the United States. Papandreou's
PASOK party had campaigned for a "multi-dimensional" foreign policy to replace Greece's supposed overdependence on the
United States. At the meeting of NATO Defense Ministers in
Brussels in December 1981, Papandreou,[9] asserting that Greece
was the only NATO member to face a threat from another
member, called on his fellow members to state formally that
NATO guarantees under Article 5 applied to threats from
within the alliance as well as from outside it. Denials by the Turks
that they were threatening Greece and complaints from other
members that, under the circumstances, passage of a resolution
like the one proposed by Papandreou would constitute a re-
proach Turkey did not merit, resulted in the defeat of the Greek

initiative. Most of the other members believed that such a pledge would add nothing to the treaty which, in any event, under Article 1, affirmed the commitment of the parties "to settle any international dispute in which they may be involved by peaceful means. . . . " Papandreou, however, refused to approve the text of a final communiqué that did not include the Greek wording. Since the communiqué required unanimous approval, the result of the impasse was that, for the first time in NATO history, no communiqué of defense ministers was issued. Greece had dramatized its position on the territorial issue but at the price of isolating itself further in the NATO council and reinforcing the determination of the NATO secretariat to steer clear of Greek-Turkish problems.

In view of Turkey's refusal to permit a reinterpretation of the scope of NATO guarantees and Greece's stated position against negotiating bilateral differences until Turkish troops leave Cyprus, what role could the alliance hope to play in helping Greece and Turkey address the issue of territorial security? The question is an important one if resolution of this issue could, as the author believes, open the way to a new Greek-Turkish détente which, in the world of the 1990s, would have a better chance to endure than the détente of 1930.

There is, in fact, a way to meet Greece's desire for NATO guarantees without offending Turkey and to take advantage of Turkey's willingness to negotiate a treaty of nonaggression without prejudice to the Greek position on Turkish troops in Cyprus. This is for NATO to inform Athens and Ankara that the alliance would be prepared to guarantee a pact of nonaggression negotiated by the two powers themselves.

Guarantees of this kind are conventional diplomatic instruments useful in lending weight and credibility to agreements that are not self-enforcing. Treaties of guarantee were customary in the nineteenth century,[10] and the provision for guarantor powers in the Zurich and London accords of 1960 was an attempt, although ultimately a failed one, to apply the concept to Cyprus. Greece, Turkey, and Great Britain were unable to "guarantee" the security of the Cypriot republic in 1974 because both Greece and Turkey—as well as the Greek and Turkish Cypriot communities—had become convinced (for very different reasons) that the 1960 Cyprus constitution was unworkable. Britain, in its capacity as the third guarantor power, might have intervened more forcefully if the United States had been willing to lend active support. Paralyzed by the escalating Watergate crisis, and with no policy objective beyond trying to limit the damage done by the 1974 Cyprus crisis to its relations with Turkey and Greece, the Nixon administration remained passive.[11]

A NATO guarantee of a Greek-Turkish nonaggression pact would be a more credible instrument of reinforcement than the three-power guarantees applied to Cyprus and would reassure both Greece and Turkey that their closest military allies were committed to safeguarding their peaceful relations. Dependent as they are on their NATO partners for military and economic assistance that could not be replaced from other sources, the Greek and Turkish governments would be unlikely to resort to tactics of intimidation in Cyprus or the Aegean and would have strong arguments to use against extremist factions advocating such policies.

While NATO has not in the past undertaken a guarantee of this kind, the initiatives of secretaries general Ismay and Spaak in 1957–1958, and the effort of the British with U.S. support in 1964 to form a peacekeeping force for Cyprus recruited from NATO member states, went much further in implicating the alliance in the problems of Greece and Turkey.[12] The proposed guarantee would focus NATO diplomacy on the most urgent aspect of the Greek-Turkish confrontation in the most politically neutral way. It would be a valuable test of NATO's ability to treat differences between its members that are not of an exclusively military nature but have direct bearing on the alliance's military readiness and political coherence.

Acting in the wholly appropriate role of an *amicus curiae,* NATO would encourage Greece and Turkey to take the lead in reducing tensions and offer them a tangible premium if they did so successfully. Turkey would enter negotiations on the same footing as Greece, not as a presumed aggressor, and would have no prima facie reason to object to NATO guaranteeing an agreement of the kind the Turkish president has said he was open to signing. Greece would achieve its avowed objective of an alliance guarantee against aggression "from any quarter" but in a form that made no political assumptions disobliging to Turkey. Both Greece and Turkey by this means would agree to set aside the threat of force in settling their differences and would associate NATO in the process of reconciliation.

Not the least of the immediate benefits to be derived from NATO-sponsored negotiations of this kind would be the opportunity they provided to reduce the occurrence of flash firefights between Greek and Turkish forces that risk getting out of control. When Turkish military exercises in the Aegean result in Turkish aircraft penetrating the ten miles of air space that Greece claims around its islands—something that has happened often and continues to occur up to the time of this writing—Greek aircraft are scrambled and the risk of a dogfight between NATO allies becomes palpable.[13] In effect, the responsibility for avoiding an incident with irreversible consequences rests with young TACAIR pilots on both sides. Nor are the dangers of Greek-Turkish hostilities confined to disputed Aegean airspace. In December 1986, one Greek and two Turkish soldiers were killed in an exchange of fire that occurred along the Evros/Maritsa River that delineates the borders of Greek and Turkish Thrace, and in March 1987 a maritime confrontation over oil exploration rights nearly caused a rupture in diplomatic relations.

In the process of negotiating a nonaggression pact to be guaranteed by NATO, it would be logical for Greece and Turkey to develop confidence-building measures and improved bilateral communications to replace those the alliance's military organization would provide if the armed forces of both sides were exercising together and the military machinery of NATO's southeastern flank were functioning normally. These would include observers at national military exercises, hot lines, advance notification of unusual military deployments, and other measures already put into place by NATO and the Warsaw Pact. We are told that after the meeting of prime ministers Özal and Papandreou in Davos in January 1988 procedures of this kind were discussed, but it is not clear what has actually been done.

The persistence of air incidents suggests that existing measures are insufficient.

It is encouraging that, despite the absence of reliable confidence-building machinery, Ankara and Athens have managed to avoid being drawn into a wider conflict in the Aegean. This is a strong indication that they do not really want to engage in hostilities and a further reason for NATO to begin quietly to explore in Athens and Ankara ways in which their evident but unexpressed commitment to peaceful solutions could be made formal and explicit.

While visiting Turkey, Greece, and Cyprus in the summer of 1990, the author and the Council on Foreign Relations's director of studies, Nicholas X. Rizopoulos, raised with Turkish and Greek officials the feasibility of negotiating a nonaggression pact to be guaranteed by NATO. In Ankara, the initial Turkish reaction was skeptical but not dismissive. Senior Turkish military officers expressed the view that such a pact would only encourage Greece to extend its territorial seas to twelve miles around the Greek islands in the Aegean, a move Turkey has publicly warned it would regard as a cause for war. When the author asked whether the concept of a nonaggression pact would be more interesting to the Turks if coupled with a Greek pledge not to extend its territorial seas to twelve miles—a right Greece claims but says it does not intend to exercise—the Turkish response was more positive, although doubts were expressed that Greece would agree to this condition. Even former prime minister Bulent Ecevit, who in the past has said that Turkey and Greece, as members of the same military alliance, needed no additional guarantees, thought that the concept was worth looking at in view of NATO's increasing emphasis on political rather than purely military goals. In Athens, Greek officials expressed the opinion that Turkey would never agree to give up the implied threat of force but acknowledged their own continuing interest in securing guarantees. At minimum, our discussions in Ankara and Athens suggested that NATO diplomacy would have something to work with if the alliance decided to replace the secretary general's "watching brief" with a more active role.

Whether the NATO council would be prepared to authorize a more active role for the secretary general can only be determined by soundings among the members, an initiative that could be quietly undertaken by the U.S. permanent representative. Those members of the council, notably the French, who have objected to NATO's assuming "out-of-area" responsibilities, could not object on these grounds to an alliance guarantee affecting the relations of two fellow members. If, however, the United States became convinced after consultation with council members that unanimous support for a NATO guarantee could not be obtained, other alternatives could be considered. A group of guarantor powers, composed of NATO members but not committing the alliance as a whole, would lend credibility to a Greek-Turkish pact of nonaggression, particularly if it included the United States. This would follow the precedent of the peace-keeping force proposed for Cyprus in 1964 but without involving NATO members directly in the affairs of a non-NATO state. Other variations are conceivable, including a guarantee by the United States alone, acting as an ally of both Greece and Turkey, and as the sea power dominant in the Mediterranean. None, however, would have the impact of a guarantee backed by the alliance as a whole, just as none would demonstrate as clearly the ability of NATO to take on new tasks in a new strategic environment in which regional instability and violence have become greater threats to peace than the clash of opposing blocs.

Twenty-two years ago, still recovering from the shock of French withdrawal from NATO's integrated military commands, and feeling, as it does today, the need to reorient its position in a changing strategic environment, the North Atlantic Council approved the Harmel Report on the "future tasks of the alliance." In its ministerial meeting in December 1967, the council observed wisely that a primary purpose of NATO was "to pursue the search for progress towards a more stable relationship in which the underlying political issues can be solved. . . . The ultimate political purpose of the alliance is to achieve a just and lasting peaceful order in Europe accompanied by appropriate security guarantees."[14]

Comments like these, designed to show that NATO's ultimate goal was détente with the Soviet Union and that this could only be achieved through a strengthened sense of national security among the members, apply just as aptly to the Greek-Turkish confrontation and suggest just as clearly the policies NATO should adopt in bringing détente to its southeastern flank. Success in restoring a sense of national security in Athens and Ankara could then, with NATO's help, embolden Greece and Turkey to address the more complicated and far-reaching issues that regularly generate military tension between the two states.

8

CYPRUS, GREECE, AND TURKEY

No issue in dispute between Greece and Turkey is more complex and far-reaching in its implications or has generated more military tension between them since they became NATO allies in 1952 than the Cyprus problem. Located in the eastern Mediterranean, outside the boundaries of the Aegean Sea, Cyprus is roughly the size of Delaware and Rhode Island combined. It is situated less than 50 miles from the southern coast of Turkey and over 500 miles from the Greek mainland. Its population numbers about 677,000, 80 percent of whom are of Greek origin, 18 percent of Turkish origin, and the remainder comprising small, mainly Christian, minorities.[1]

Cyprus is an independent, nonaligned state which was admitted to the United Nations in 1960, the year it achieved independence from Great Britain. As a result of the Zurich and London accords of 1959–1960 that ended the status of Cyprus as a British Crown colony, an immensely complicated system of checks and balances was written into the new state's constitution by the Greek, Turkish, and British negotiators with the intention of safeguarding the rights of the Turkish Cypriot minority while enabling Cyprus to function as a unitary state.[2] At the same time, despite Cyprus's nonaligned status, Great Britain retained sovereign control over two military base areas and the use of numerous "retained sites" elsewhere in the southern part of the island. Although none of these facilities has a specifically NATO-assigned mission, they support Western, including NATO, interests by virtue of the electronic intelligence capability that has been installed there by the British and U.S. governments. The sovereign base areas have also proved a valuable and sometimes essential means of supporting the UN force serving in Cyprus and have played a role in various Near Eastern contingencies, notably in Lebanon in 1982 and the Sinai since 1980.

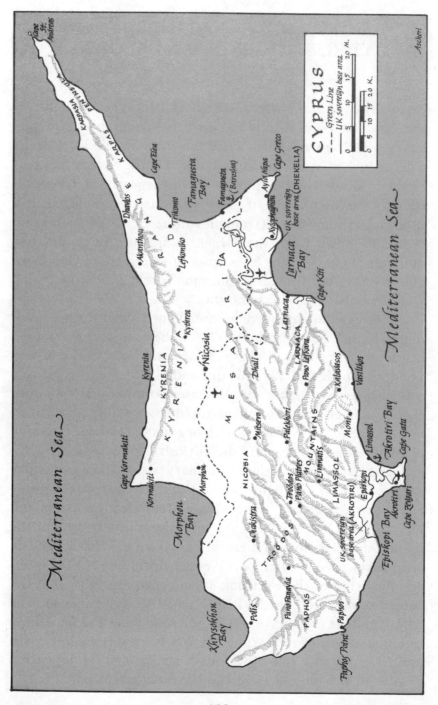

As we saw in chapter 2, Britain undertook the negotiations that led in 1960 to the independence of Cyprus with great reluctance. The negotiating process begun in London in 1955 was conducted primarily with Greece and Turkey rather than with the Cypriots themselves. The British government knew that the road to a Cyprus settlement led through Athens and Ankara. Neither the Greeks nor the Turks, it should be noted, were pressing for Cypriot independence. Greece sought *enosis*—the unification of Cyprus with Greece—and Turkey sought to preserve the status quo or, failing that, favored *taksim*—the partition of Cyprus between the two motherlands. These incompatible objectives were also favored over independence by the island's ethnic communities.

Thus, when independence was finally achieved after arduous negotiations over the space of five years, it represented a less than satisfactory compromise for all the parties concerned. Cyprus must be the only member state of the United Nations for which national independence was only a consolation prize.

While a kind of Cypriot nationalism has developed over time, it has a curiously muted quality, which suggests that the two communities still see themselves first as Greeks and Turks and only secondarily as Cypriots. The fact that independent Cyprus has never adopted a national anthem and that Greek and Turkish flags have always been as conspicuous there as the flag of Cyprus—itself a compromise whose design, a silhouette of the island in yellow against a white field, seems less designed to inspire patriotism than to avoid offense—permits the same inference.[3]

The absence of a sense of national identity helps explain why Cyprus is still a divided island almost two decades after the Greek junta opened the door to Turkish military intervention by attempting to achieve *enosis* through an unsuccessful coup d'état against the elected president of Cyprus, Archbishop Makarios, and his replacement by a fanatically anti-Turkish terrorist Nikos Sampson. Given the fact that the Greek and Turkish Cypriot populations were intermingled throughout the island when Turkish troops landed on the north coast in July 1974, the ensuing hostilities might well have turned into a protracted civil war instead of a war of separation had the two communities not regrouped—Turkish Cypriots moving north to seek the protection of the intervening Turkish forces, Greek Cypriots moving south to escape them.

The human cost of this displacement of populations was terrible—over 160,000 Greek Cypriots abandoned their homes in the north and about 65,000 Turkish Cypriots did the same in the south—but it did facilitate the task of the UN peacekeeping force in creating a buffer zone—along the so-called Green Line established by the British in 1963–1964—to separate the two ethnic groups. One can only speculate what the situation would have been had the two communities fought each other as rival Cypriot clans rather than as Greeks and Turks living in Cyprus. It is likely that the struggle would have been even bloodier and the two sides even more difficult to separate, as in Lebanon.

Today some 30,000 Turkish troops remain in occupation of the northern 36 percent of Cyprus, including the picturesque ports of Kyrenia and Famagusta, formerly magnets for European tourism, and agricultural land, especially citrus groves, that is the most fertile on the island. Despite these advantages, the economy of northern Cyprus, weakened by the embargo imposed on the north in 1974 by the Republic of Cyprus and by the consequent difficulty the Turkish Cypriots have experienced in marketing exports, attracting investment, and training a generally unskilled labor force, has lagged behind that of the south. Since only Ankara has recognized the Turkish Republic of Northern Cyprus declared in November 1983, the north has been obliged to adopt the Turkish lira as its currency and depend almost exclusively on Turkey for investment, financial aid, and tourism. This forced dependency has saddled northern Cyprus with many of the economic problems of the Turkish motherland, including an inflation rate of over 50 percent annually. Although the economy of the north has been growing at an estimated annual rate of 6 percent or more, the per capita income of the Turkish Cypriots is still only $2,000, about one-fourth that of the Greek Cypriots.[4]

The southern 64 percent of the island controlled by the Republic of Cyprus has in the past ten years developed a boom-

ing economy, mainly energized by tourism and foreign com-
panies that were driven out of Beirut by the fighting there and
have found a hospitable second home in Cyprus, where they can
maintain their access to the Middle East. With an annual growth
rate of 6–8 percent during the past five years, and a per capita
income of $8,000, the Republic of Cyprus has not only resettled
the refugees from the north and virtually eliminated unemploy-
ment but has achieved a level of prosperity that exceeds that of
Greece itself. Ironically, southern Cyprus suffers from a short-
age of labor that could easily and profitably be supplied by the
north if the island were not divided. In fact, the author was
told—on his visit to Cyprus in the summer of 1990—that "black-
market" labor from the north was being employed by Greek
Cypriot enterprises near the Green Line. This is not the only sad
anomaly produced by the de facto partition of Cyprus.

The unwillingness of the communities to shed their Greek
and Turkish identities, and in so doing to shed the historic
quarrels of their motherlands, has made Cyprus the United
Nations' costliest peacekeeping operation after the Middle East
and its longest uninterrupted peacekeeping operation after
Kashmir. And even Kashmir has not been the object of such
sustained diplomatic therapy by the UN secretary general. Despite his efforts since 1968, and the repeated blessings bestowed
on them by the Security Council, the two communities have
grown farther and farther apart. When Secretary General Javier
Pérez de Cuéllar inaugurated a new round of intercommunal
talks on February 26, 1990, he invited the communities to "approach [their] task [of negotiations] not face to face but side to
side." They were unable to do so and the new round failed, like so
many before it. The reason was inescapably clear. Face to face the
two communities are Greek and Turkish; side by side they would
be Cypriot.

The question of how Greek and Turkish Cypriots see themselves is important because it helps to determine which of several
possible negotiating strategies is most likely to restore to Cyprus
its national integrity and remove it as a bone of contention
between Greece and Turkey. Three lines of approach are theo-
retically possible:

• A package approach—Cyprus can be treated as a problem so entangled in the skein of Greek-Turkish differences that it cannot be negotiated apart from them. If this assumption is correct, an overall package settlement should be the goal, and Greece and Turkey must be brought directly into the negotiating process.

• A framework approach—Cyprus can be regarded as a problem whose solution will require Greek and Turkish agreement but not that Athens and Ankara simultaneously resolve all their other differences, some of which, like the Aegean shelf issue, will involve impartial adjudication that could extend over a longer time than the Cyprus problem should be allowed to fester. In this approach, the goal would be to persuade Greece and Turkey to initial a framework agreement defining their own Cypriot interests and the general principles they believe must be embodied in an accord between the communities and committing them to support the efforts of the communities to achieve an agreement respecting these interests and principles. Within this framework, the two communities, under the auspices of the UN secretary general, could work out detailed constitutional and territorial arrangements. Bilateral Greek-Turkish problems could then be addressed by Athens and Ankara free of the friction and distrust engendered by the Cyprus dispute.

• An intercommunal approach—Cyprus can be approached as a problem that is essentially the responsibility of the two communities to resolve. The interests of Athens and Ankara can be construed to be a function of their domestic political agendas and therefore secondary to the real interests of the two Cypriot communities—which, after all, will actually have to live with whatever solution is negotiated. This approach assumes that if the two Cypriot communities can be induced to agree on a set of constitutional and territorial compromises, Greece and Turkey will not be in a position to block its implementation.

The intercommunal negotiations (or "talks" as they are more often called) that have been conducted through the offices of the UN secretary general since 1968, albeit with frequent and sometimes extended interruptions, basically represent the third of the three approaches outlined above. Although the Greek and

Turkish governments have been asked from time to time to intercede with the two communities in the interest of keeping the talks going, they have not been brought directly into the negotiating process and have not, since 1971, expressed themselves jointly on the subject of a Cyprus settlement. Let us therefore look at what the intercommunal negotiations have achieved so far, the features that have characterized them, and, in particular, the roles played by Greece and Turkey in the negotiating process.

Formal talks between the two communities were begun in June 1968, following the intercommunal violence at the end of the previous year that had caused the Johnson administration to launch the Vance mission[5] in November in order to prevent Turkish military intervention in Cyprus and avert the threat of a war between Greece and Turkey. Relations between the communities had been exacerbated by the return to Cyprus from Greece in 1966 of the same Colonel (by then General) George Grivas whose leadership of the EOKA guerrillas ten years earlier had aimed at unification of Cyprus with Greece but had resulted instead in independence.[6] Grivas himself had never abandoned his dream of *enosis,* and when the Vance mission succeeded in persuading the Turks to refrain from military intervention, two of Ankara's conditions were the departure of Grivas from the island and the commencement of talks between the communities to improve the functioning of the 1960 Cypriot constitution.

This first period of intercommunal talks lasted from 1968 to 1974 and was divided into two phases. In the first phase (1968–1972) the Greek and Turkish Cypriot representatives, Glafkos Clerides and Rauf Denktash, met in the presence of the UN secretary general's special representative in Cyprus, acting in the capacity of an observer. When the talks deadlocked in 1971, the second phase began in June of the next year with the active participation of the special representative, as well as that of a Greek and a Turkish constitutional expert.

It is interesting—and not without significance—that the 1971 deadlock was only broken after exchanges between Greek and Turkish representatives held in Lisbon during the May 1971 meeting of NATO foreign ministers. As a result of these corridor meetings, the Greek and Turkish governments, as the British writer Robert McDonald puts it,

> agreed to promote continuation of the intercommunal talks, but along lines laid down by Athens and Ankara. In exchange for the Turkish Cypriots accepting a number of [President] Makarios' constitutional amendments, it was proposed that they should have a cabinet minister with extensive authority over local government. Both sides reaffirmed the [1959–1960] London and Zurich accords, and Turkey, reiterating its adherence to the Treaty of Guarantee, undertook not to invade Cyprus without prior consultation with Athens. The two governments agreed that if the talks failed to resolve the problem they would act jointly to impose a "definitive solution" though they apparently differed about the form this might take.[7]

On the Turkish side, renewed support for the intercommunal talks was facilitated by the emergence of a new government in Ankara. In March 1971, the Turkish military had installed as prime minister the veteran Turkish diplomat, Nihat Erim, who had been directly involved in negotiating the 1960 Cyprus constitution. On the Greek side, the picture was (as it usually is) a bit murkier, but historians of the Colonels' junta that ruled Greece from 1967 to 1974 agree that, in 1971, Prime Minister George Papadopoulos began a policy of limited "liberalization" that involved the release of 250 political prisoners, as well as an attempt to enter into communications with a select group of political personalities with a view to winning their cooperation.[8] Papadopoulos hoped by this means to improve the junta's image in Western Europe and the United States. A change in the junta's external policy had the same objective. Papadopoulos wished to demonstrate that Greece, under its military regime, was a steadfast NATO ally. The best way to convey this impression was to make a gesture of friendship to Turkey, and the best place to do so was at the forthcoming NATO foreign ministers' meeting in Lisbon.

The accounts that both Greek Cypriot and Turkish Cypriot observers have given of the second phase of the intercommunal talks indicate that substantial progress was made in the 1971– 1972 period. One Turkish Cypriot writer reports that "differences of the two sides on the Executive and the Judiciary were narrowed, complete agreement was reached on the legislature, and even on the thorny problem of local government substantial progress was made."[9] The Greek Cypriot negotiator, Glafkos Clerides, four years later (in 1976) revealed publicly that a "near" agreement had been reached which he had unsuccessfully urged the Cyprus Council of Ministers to accept.[10]

This may be the closest the two communities have come to an agreement since the 1960 constitutional arrangements broke down at the end of 1963. Athens and Ankara wanted a settlement, or at least said they did, and the negotiators thought they had the elements of one in hand. What happened, then, to cause this opportunity to be lost?

The responsibility lies with the Greek government and can be traced to tensions within the Athens junta between soft- and hard-liners, those like Papadopoulos, who favored some accommodation with Turkey in order to propitiate the United States and NATO, and those like security chief Dimitrios Ioannides, who adamantly opposed accommodation (and two years later, in the fall of 1973, deposed Papadopoulos). In May 1971, within three months of the time that the Greek government had reaffirmed its support for the Zurich and London accords, General Grivas, who had supposedly been under house arrest in Athens after withdrawing from Cyprus in 1967, slipped out of Greece and returned to the island. This could only have happened with the complicity of the Greek government. It suggests either that hard-liners within the junta were seeking to counteract the Papadopoulos initiative or that the Greek prime minister himself allowed Grivas to escape as a sop to the hard-liners.

Whatever the explanation, the effect of Grivas's return to Cyprus, where he set about organizing the so-called EOKA-B movement to renew the struggle for unification with Greece, was to reduce President Makarios's room for maneuvering and stiffen his position in the intercommunal talks. The question of greater autonomy for the Turkish Cypriots was especially sensitive since it could create resistance to the Clerides-Denktash agreement among Greek Cypriots and add fuel to Grivas's campaign for *enosis*. The continuing presence of Grivas on Cyprus until his death in January 1974, and his openly expressed hostility to Makarios, greatly complicated the course of the intercommunal talks, which finally were ruptured in the summer of 1974 by the junta-inspired coup against Makarios and Turkey's subsequent military intervention. The drastically altered balance of power on the island that resulted from these developments has profoundly affected the character of the talks ever since.

What emerges from this account of the circumstances surrounding the 1968–1974 intercommunal talks is that the Greek Cypriot and Turkish Cypriot negotiators were capable of reaching agreement on both constitutional and territorial issues only as long as Greece and Turkey were prepared actively to support the negotiating process. As soon as one of the motherlands— Greece in this case—began to hedge its support, the talks deadlocked.

When contacts between the communities were haltingly resumed in 1975, again under the auspices of the UN secretary general, the agenda had changed and the two sides were farther apart then ever. The Turkish Cypriots henceforth would be guided by the desire to demonstrate that the 1960 constitution was dead and, with it, the prospect of reviving a unitary state, the Greek Cypriots by the desire to gain the withdrawal of Turkish troops and the restoration of the central government's authority throughout Cyprus. Efforts by the Turkish Cypriots to strengthen their negotiating position by claiming the prerogatives of statehood, first, in 1975, as the Turkish Federated State of Cyprus, later, in 1983, as the Turkish Republic of Northern Cyprus, have been countered by Nicosia and Athens with UN resolutions affirming the sovereignty and territorial integrity of the Cypriot Republic, admonishing other states to recognize no other Cypriot entity, and calling for the withdrawal of Turkish forces. None of these developments has enhanced the prospects for the intercommunal talks or facilitated the task of the UN secretary general, who has found his mandate harder and harder to discharge.

Indeed, as positions have congealed since 1974, the secretary general has been obliged to take more responsibility on himself for keeping the intercommunal talks alive. Where few outside observers could discern any common elements or hopeful signs, the secretary general has adduced "indicators" of agreement (1983), or proposed a five-point "scenario" and a set of "working points" (1984), or finally prepared a "draft framework agreement on Cyprus" (1986). In this process, the ingenuity of the secretary general in defining grounds for agreement has been exceeded only by that of the communities in finding reasons not to agree. The cost of these failed initiatives has been twofold: Each failure reduces the leverage that the secretary general has for subsequent initiatives, and each exposes him to direct criticism from one or both sides. After the collapse of the January 1985 intercommunal "summit," which the secretary general and his staff had made heroic diplomatic efforts to arrange, Pérez de Cuéllar was attacked by the Turks for revising with the Greek Cypriots a draft agreement that the Turkish Cypriots claimed had already been approved by both sides. The same ill-fated initiative produced a charge by the Cyprus government that UN officials were guilty of "paternalism."[11]

Clearly, the intercommunal process has gone about as far as it can go without the addition of some new element. Equally clearly, the secretary general's prestige has been stretched to the breaking point in trying to bridge differences that the two communities, backed to the hilt by their motherlands, are unwilling or unable to reconcile by negotiation. Nothing that has occurred since the flurry of activity during 1985–1986 gives cause for optimism that the intercommunal talks will by themselves produce a solution to the problems of Cyprus, whatever the exertions of the secretary general. Athens and Ankara will have to be induced to play a more constructive role if the basis of a new settlement is to be found—the kind of role they first played in 1959–1960 and later, more briefly in 1971–1972.

This leads us back to the alternative approaches we outlined earlier: the package approach, treating Cyprus as a problem inseparable from other Greek-Turkish disputes and therefore best negotiated as one component of a larger package; and the framework approach, treating Cyprus as a problem that the two communities will only be able to negotiate if Greece and Turkey themselves first agree on the basic framework for such a settlement.

The objection immediately raised by the first of these alternatives—the package approach—is that if Greece and Turkey are unable to agree on sea and air space issues, the Aegean continental shelf, military command-and-control arrangements, and other persistent bilateral problems, why would adding Cyprus to the agenda improve the prospects for a settlement? Advocates of the package approach say that more trade-offs, and therefore more compromises, would be possible. How, they ask, could Cyprus be put to one side while bilateral problems are being negotiated? It is the area where Greek-Turkish conflicts have been the most visible to the outside world and where the United Nations has been forced to take a position and to place a peacekeeping force. Its very visibility guarantees that as long as the Greeks and Turks are unable to agree about Cyprus they will be unable to agree about anything else. So runs the argument made by those favoring a comprehensive settlement, who also point out that the most successful negotiation of Greek-Turkish problems in this century was accomplished at Lausanne in 1923 under cover of a package agreement that resolved not only Turkey's most important bilateral differences with Greece but also those with the other Entente powers in the wake of World War I.[12]

This line of reasoning is compatible with the call by the Republic of Cyprus and Greece for an international conference on Cyprus but not with strong Turkish objections to participating in a conference where they might find themselves as isolated as they have been in the UN General Assembly. The United States has also consistently opposed the idea, largely because Washington saw it as an invitation to the Soviet Union to promote further dissension between two NATO allies and to increase Soviet influence in Cyprus, where the Moscow-line Communist party is the strongest single party on the island. The U.S. government has been especially reluctant to concede to Moscow a voice in renegotiating the Zurich and London accords and thereby risk the closure of the British sovereign base areas. These objections may become less important in the new international climate, where détente between the United States and the Soviet Union has been achieved before détente between Greece and Turkey.

As we saw in chapter 4, the Soviet Union has already played an active role in finessing the Greek-Turkish dispute over Mersin in the context of the conventional arms talks. Nevertheless, an international conference on Cyprus would be a major and a risky undertaking which, by forcing the participants to negotiate in the spotlight of public or semipublic diplomacy, could lead them to harden their positions and leave the situation worse than before if the conference were to fail. Exactly because the Republic of Cyprus is sovereign and has its own voice in the United Nations, and because constitutional and territorial problems affecting the two communities are qualitatively different from the bilateral problems of Greece and Turkey, it is hard to see how all could be effectively addressed at an international conference. Before attempting so ambitious a venture, it seems logical to try using a smaller forum with a less complicated agenda.

NATO is such a forum, and a less complicated agenda could still include the negotiation of agreed Greek and Turkish guidelines for a Cyprus settlement, along the lines of the third alternative—the framework agreement. If our reading of events at the meeting of NATO foreign ministers in Lisbon in 1971 is correct, this is what happened there. The ensuing collapse of negotiations, however, indicates the shortcomings of this approach. The Cyprus problem remains a hostage to other Greek-Turkish issues, and a change of policy in either Greece or Turkey quickly invalidates any framework agreement to which they have subscribed. Thus, one is left with the logical inference that Greek-Turkish distrust is as much the cause as the effect of the Cyprus problem.

This is easily checked against the record of failed diplomacy in Cyprus and the Aegean since 1974. Periods of relative détente in Greek-Turkish relations have usually led to periods of détente on the island, periods of tension between Athens and Ankara to deteriorating relations, if not to actual armed conflict, between the two Cypriot communities. Often, changes in the texture of Greek-Turkish relations are simply the result of domestic political developments in both countries, usually the approach of parliamentary elections. So sensitively tuned are the Greek and Turkish Cypriot communities to the prevailing political winds from Athens and Ankara, that no change in the temperature of Greek-Turkish relations is too subtle to register on intercommunal relations in Cyprus and on the negotiating process pursued by the office of the UN secretary general.

In May 1975, for example, prime ministers Constantine Karamanlis and Suleyman Demirel, seeking to put behind them the tragic events of the previous summer, met in Brussels to declare their support for the intercommunal talks that resumed in Vienna in July with renewed hopes of progress. By September, Demirel began feeling the heat from his domestic opposition. His position then stiffened on both bilateral issues and Cyprus. Soon thereafter, the New York round of the intercommunal talks, scheduled for the same month, was canceled. The talks were resumed in Vienna in February 1976, but a series of Greek-Turkish confrontations over air space and the Aegean shelf intervened. The Vienna phase of the intercommunal talks ended in 1977 after six fruitless rounds.

By the beginning of 1978, a new Turkish government headed by Bulent Ecevit had declared its intention to get the talks started again and implied its willingness to be flexible. The Turkish gesture, which was made with the urging of the United States, was motivated in large part by the desire of the Turkish and U.S. governments to show progress in Cyprus and thus ease the way for Congress to lift the Turkish arms embargo. This, of course, was the very step that Athens and Nicosia wanted most to forestall. Thereupon, the Greek and Greek Cypriot position hardened perceptibly and the new Turkish proposals were rejected (although the embargo was in any case lifted in September 1978).

The same pattern can be observed in the so-called Ledra Palace talks between August 1980 and March 1983.[13] The former U.S. ambassador to Turkey, James W. Spain, has described how the U.S. government decided in early 1980 to provide impetus to the intercommunal talks that Washington feared were about to break down completely.[14] Because Washington's strategy was (and remains) to shelter behind the UN secretary general and to respond to critics of U.S. policy by pointing to hoped-for, but thus far illusory, signs of progress in the intercommunal talks, their collapse in 1980 would have been viewed as a sharp setback for U.S. diplomacy.

U.S. efforts to promote flexibility were complicated on the Turkish side by a military takeover in Ankara in September 1980. Thus, when Ambassador Spain approached Turkey's new military leaders shortly after they had assumed power and conveyed Washington's plea for greater flexibility, their response was that domestic problems had to be addressed first before Turkey could turn its attention to the Cyprus problem. Not until March 1981 was Ankara prepared to consider any new proposals for the intercommunal talks, and not until August of that year did the Turks actually submit a proposal to withdraw their military forces to an area of Cyprus reduced from 36 percent to 30 percent of the island's territory.

It was, once again, too little too late. "Unfortunately, the [conservative] New Democracy government in Athens under Prime Minister Rallis was not prepared to pick up the Turkish offer," Spain notes sadly. "New elections were due in Greece in October [1981]; the political consequences of any move on Cyprus were uncertain; further movement was postponed until after the elections."[15] Any prospects for progress in the intercommunal talks had once again been subordinated to the domestic political preoccupations of Athens and Ankara. Moreover, the Greek elections of October 1981 brought to power a new and assertively nationalist government under Prime Minister Andreas Papandreou, one of whose first actions was to break off the working-level meetings with Ankara that had been going on with regularity ever since 1975. As noted, there has been little subsequent progress made in the intercommunal talks, and the efforts of the UN secretary general to keep them going have earned him no gratitude from the participants.

Small wonder then that former UN under secretary general Brian Urquhart has said of Cyprus, "I know of no problem more frustrating or more bedeviled by mean-spiritedness and lack of mutual confidence, nor of any problem where all concerned would so obviously gain from a reasonable settlement."[16] More precisely, where all concerned would so obviously gain in the long run. In the short run, it is exactly the expediency of not agreeing that accounts for the continuing failure to achieve a reasonable settlement.

On the island itself, the Turkish Cypriot leader, Rauf Denktash, has the most to lose personally if he exchanges the perquisites of phantom sovereignty for the perilous leadership of an embattled minority in a reunified Cypriot republic. In a meeting with Denktash in Nicosia in July 1990, both the author and his colleague from the Council on Foreign Relations detected little give in the Turkish Cypriot leader's position. In the course of an animated discussion of more than an hour's duration with Denktash and a group of his advisors, he argued strongly for international recognition of northern Cyprus and maintained that Turkish Cypriots would accept no solution that did not accord them equal rights under a new constitution. Referring to the "three freedoms"—freedom of movement, settlement, and ownership of property—that the Greek Cypriots believe are essential to a final settlement, Denktash said that his community would insist on specific safeguards to prevent the Turkish Cypriot zone from being "infiltrated and overwhelmed" by the more numerous and wealthier Greek Cypriots. When the author suggested that the status quo was inherently unstable since it required a costly UN peacekeeping force to sustain it, Denktash retorted, "Let the UN troops leave. We don't need them." [17]

Our conversations with other Turkish Cypriot representatives, especially those concerned with the problems of the northern sector's economy, suggested that movement in this area may be possible and should precede negotiations over political differences. The need to reintegrate the island's economy is compelling in its own right. Not only is northern labor needed in the south, but island-wide development of tourism would profit Greek and Turkish Cypriots alike. The island's declining water supply is shared between north and south, and the Republic of Cyprus continues to supply the north with electricity, but with the passage of time, if no economic reunification occurs, northern Cyprus will inevitably come to depend more and more on Turkey. The republic's embargo is already having this unintended and undesirable effect. The author was told while visiting

Cyprus of projects, like a cellular telephone system for northern Cyprus, that the Turkish Cypriots were obliged by the embargo to integrate with Turkey, although their preference was for an island-wide system.

The Greek Cypriots have less to lose from a settlement of the Cyprus problem, but the concessions they will probably have to make to achieve it—credible constitutional guarantees to the Turkish minority and acceptance of a bizonal federation (or confederation)—invariably appear politically too hazardous to accept. As early as 1972, as we have seen, this was the judgment of President Makarios, whose prestige among all sectors of the Greek Cypriot community was unrivaled. It has also been, more understandably, that of the relatively weaker coalition governments that have succeeded him. Even the election to the presidency, in February 1988, of George Vassiliou—a new face on the political scene of the Republic of Cyprus who is not a professional politician but a successful businessman and a person believed to be more pragmatic than his predecessor, Spyros Kyprianou—has not supplied the impetus to the intercommunal talks that many hoped it would. Our own meeting with Vassiliou in Nicosia, in July 1990, showed him to be articulate and personable but visibly discouraged by the collapse of the UN secretary general's latest initiative earlier that spring. Vassiliou seemed particularly frustrated by the difficulty he has encountered in convincing outside observers that, under his presidency, the Republic of Cyprus accepts Turkish Cypriots as equals and wants to give them fair treatment under a new constitution. He was outraged by the complaint voiced by Denktash and various Ankara officials that the republic's July 1990 application for full membership in the European Community should have been cleared first with the Turkish Cypriot community. "We are making this application on behalf of all Cypriots," Vassiliou said, noting that EC disbursements to Cyprus as an associate member were being shared with the northern sector. Like our Turkish Cypriot interlocutors, Vassiliou seemed to think that economic cooperation between the two communities might be easier to achieve than political cooperation.

In fact, the broad outlines of what a final settlement of Cypriot intercommunal problems will look like have been clear for a long time. Pérez de Cuéllar seems to have annoyed both sides by spelling them out. In his statement to the two community leaders made in February 1990, the UN secretary general said,

> Cyprus is the common home of the Greek Cypriot community and of the Turkish Cypriot community. Their relationship is not one of majority and minority, but one of two communities in the State of Cyprus. . . . The two communities have, in the 1979 high-level agreement [between Kyprianou and Denktash], specifically rejected as options union in whole or in part with any other country and any form of partition or secession. The two communities have stated that they wish to establish a federation that is bi-communal as regards the constitutional aspects and bi-zonal as regards the territorial aspects.[18]

He went on to present a detailed list of "ideas" that he said had previously "been explored with each of [the communities] on a non-committal basis" and which, by implication, he believed they could, through further negotiation, incorporate in a final settlement. The secretary general considered that agreement was within reach on the issues of "political equality . . . and the bicommunal nature of the federation"; bizonality within a unified state; the powers and functions of the federal government; the fundamental rights of citizens, including the three freedoms; security arrangements for the two communities; territorial adjustments; and displaced persons. From earlier exchanges with and between the communities, Pérez de Cuéllar defined the parameters within which each of these issues could be resolved. His remarks made it clear that the character of the new Cypriot constitution and the principles it must embody were known to the two communities and, in large part, accepted by them.

On the basis of the secretary general's analysis one conclusion is inescapable. The failure of the communities to reach agreement is caused less by the complexity of the constitutional and territorial problems they face than by their misgivings about sharing power and the disinclination of Athens and Ankara to work actively for a settlement. Time is not on the side of accommodation. As the two Cypriot communities develop their own economic infrastructures, reasons for economic cooperation will become less compelling. Furthermore, the ethnic conflicts in Yugoslavia and the Soviet Union, as well as the stubborn constitutional problems of such long-established bicommunal states as Belgium and Canada are unlikely to rekindle in Greek and Turkish Cypriots a spirit of compromise and cooperation that was grudging in the first place.

Lacking a strong desire for meaningful compromise, or a strong external impetus toward agreement, Greek and Turkish Cypriots will always have better reasons for not rocking the boat than for trying to sail it with a mixed crew. So will the United States—as long as Washington can hide behind the UN secretary general while arguing that we need no Cyprus policy other than support for the intercommunal talks. Yet, after almost a quarter of a century of such talks under cover of a UN peacekeeping force that has been in place for 26 years at a cost of over $2 billion,[19] it should have become clear that a more imaginative and courageous U.S. policy was long overdue.[20] The United States, as much as Britain and NATO, is the beneficiary of sophisticated military support and intelligence-gathering facilities on Cyprus that serve enduring Western security interests in the eastern Mediterranean, the Middle East, and North Africa. In addition, the United States has Federal Broadcast Information Service [21] antennae located on the island. These are installations that the U.S. policy of benign neglect may not endanger in the short term but has done nothing to protect in the long term.

The intent of past U.S. policy toward Cyprus might be described as creating a sense of motion without going anywhere. Since the Turkish arms embargo was lifted in 1978, the Carter, Reagan, and Bush administrations have been legislatively bound to submit bimonthly reports to Congress certifying that "progress" is being made toward a Cyprus settlement.[22] If this congressional stipulation was thought sufficient to assure as well an active U.S. role in promoting a solution to the Cyprus problem, the expectation remains largely unfulfilled. There has been no progress; yet no bimonthly presidential report has failed to detect some sign of it.

To take a relatively recent but characteristic example, President Reagan's April 21, 1987, report to the speaker of the house and the chairman of the Senate Foreign Relations Committee captures the flavor of noncommittal commitment that distinguishes these utterances. This particular report was made a month after the eruption of a major confrontation in the Aegean between Greece and Turkey in March 1987 that nearly brought them to a state of war. Indications that Greece might be planning to explore for oil in an area of the northern Aegean east of the island of Thasos, which Turkey considers to be international waters, led the Turks to prepare to launch a research vessel of their own into the same area. In the ensuing crisis, the Papandreou government sought to suspend operations at the U.S. base at Nea Makri, which at that time provided the Sixth Fleet with its land-based communications.[23] This move was intended to reflect Greek doubts that the United States would remain neutral in the event of hostilities between Greece and Turkey. The ensuing diplomatic exchanges between Athens and Ankara seemed to compound, rather than dispel, misunderstandings about their respective motives and intentions in the Aegean. The United States and NATO were then obliged to intervene and persuade Prime Minister Özal to issue instructions for the Turkish ship to stay outside the disputed area. The crisis was contained, but only by the last-minute intervention of Washington and Brussels.

Against this stormy background, President Reagan's report to Congress confined itself to a bland account of the UN secretary general's efforts to "restore momentum" to the intercommunal talks in February and March and made no mention of the near hostilities of the two parent countries. The president concluded:

> As of this date [April 21, 1987], U.N. Secretariat officials are continuing their contacts with the two sides on the proposal advanced [by the Secretary-General's representative]. In both public statements and private discussions during this period, Administration officials have stressed our continuing support for the U.N. Secretary-General's Cyprus mission. We have also been urging those directly involved with the Cyprus issue to seek every opportunity to improve the atmosphere on the island so as to enhance the prospects for progress toward a negotiated settlement.[24]

The United States, in short, was prepared to intervene to avert outright hostilities between Greece and Turkey (and to keep the base at Nea Makri operational) but was more than happy to leave the Cyprus problem in the hands of the UN secretary general and to cultivate the impression that prospects for his success were unrelated to the level of tension between the two motherlands. NATO, as we have seen, has been equally disinclined to involve itself in any long-range initiative to resolve underlying Greek-Turkish issues. The result has been stalemate in the Aegean and stalemate in Cyprus.

Well-intentioned though they may be, and as skillful and indefatigable as the diplomatic efforts of the UN Secretariat have been (as well as those of a series of energetic State Department "Special Cyprus Coordinators" in support of the secretary general), it is hard to escape the conclusion that the UN-sponsored intercommunal talks will remain fruitless until Athens and Ankara are ready to see them succeed. Furthermore, the secretary general's efforts relieve the United States of the need to adopt more realistic and effective Aegean and Cyprus policies than those Washington has been following for over twenty years. Brian Urquhart is probably right when he says resignedly of the intercommunal talks, "Perhaps the best that can be said of them is that they are like the gyroscopic stabilizer on a ship in a storm. They go round and round and produce a certain stability, even if they do not produce forward motion."[25] The worst that can be said of them is that the intercommunal talks actually have the effect of perpetuating the unhappy status quo because they enable the United States and NATO—the only powers capable of providing the prerequisites for a lasting Cyprus settlement—consistently to avoid their responsibility to do so.

If the intercommunal talks process is insufficient, if an overall package settlement is beyond reach, if a Greek-Turkish framework agreement is inherently too fragile to endure, the conclusion is inescapable that a successful resolution of the Cyprus problem must await progress on bilateral Greek-Turkish problems and a definite improvement in Greek-Turkish relations. There is ample evidence to indicate that Athens and Ankara know where their vital interests conflict and that the primary arena is not Cyprus. As a Turkish scholar observes, "Turkey's interest in Cyprus is, in essence, a response to the situation in the Aegean. An extension of Greek sovereignty to Cyprus through *enosis* would substantially enlarge the maritime area under Greek control."[26] For Greece, too, Cyprus is essentially an extension of its confrontation with Turkey in the Aegean and, because of its remoteness from the Greek mainland, a particularly inconvenient theater of potential military conflict. (We have already seen how in 1974 the Greek government was unable to offer effective military support to the Republic of Cyprus when Turkish forces landed on the island.) If de facto partition of Cyprus were to harden into something more permanent and become permanently divisive, Greece and Turkey could find themselves drawn into hostilities that would be costly and destabilizing whether they advanced or withdrew. Their military forces on the island would become hostages difficult to reinforce or remove. Logistics would favor the Turkish position, but all other factors, not least that of international legitimacy, would favor the Greeks.

Athens and Ankara have lived with the Cypriot stalemate long enough to know its inherent dangers even if they are unable—for domestic political reasons—to extricate themselves from it. Behind Turkey's public support for "self-determination" for the Turkish Cypriots and Greece's contention that no Cyprus settlement is possible until all Turkish troops have left Cyprus, the private positions of the two motherlands are more pragmatic and more flexible. Given a measure of restored mutual confidence and the incentive to promote, rather than obstruct, a settlement, the Greek and Turkish governments would assuredly accept almost any compromise acceptable to the two communities. Moreover, their influence over the two communities—greater in the case of Ankara than of Athens, but about equal in proportion to the resistance to be overcome—could be then employed to enlarge, rather than limit, the margins for compromise.

Restored mutual confidence between Greece and Turkey, as we saw in the preceding chapter, can best be instilled by the negotiation of a nonaggression pact guaranteed by NATO. The incentive for Greece and Turkey actively to promote a settlement of the Cyprus problem can only be supplied by progress toward the resolution of their bilateral differences, especially in the Aegean. Here, too, the United States and NATO have potentially valuable roles to play, ones that would reinforce the efforts of the UN secretary general and add weight to those of the Special Cyprus Coordinator. It is now time to look at these bilateral disputes more carefully and suggest ways in which Greece and Turkey could be encouraged to begin the process of reconciliation.

9

NAVIGATING THE AEGEAN PROBLEM

During their visit to Turkey, Greece, and Cyprus in the summer of 1990, the author and the Council's director of studies discussed with a large number of Turkish and Greek officials their perceptions of the changing regional security environment and how it would affect Greek and Turkish relations with the United States and with each other. It was evident in Ankara and Athens that significant rethinking of defense priorities was occurring. Although the visit took place shortly before the Iraqi invasion and occupation of Kuwait in August 1990, and Turkey and Greece were no more aware of the impending crisis than the United States, the role that each country could play in the Middle East was a definite preoccupation in both capitals. Turkish officials seemed concerned that, with the end of the Cold War, Turkey's strategic importance to the United States, and consequently its diplomatic leverage in Washington, would diminish. In the minds of the Turks, this could lead not only to sharply reduced allocations of U.S. military and economic assistance but to greater Greek influence over U.S. policy on issues affecting Turkish interests. We were told repeatedly that, as NATO's only Moslem member, Turkey would have an important role to play in promoting stability in the Middle East and mutually beneficial economic relations between the West and the Arab world. Behind these words seemed to be the assumption that if the United States had failed to appreciate fully the importance of Turkey as an ally when East-West tensions were high, Ankara could expect even less sympathy now that they had abated. We found ourselves reassuring the Turks that as long as the geography of the region remained unchanged, so would Turkey's geostrategic importance.[1] The outbreak of the Persian Gulf crisis shortly after our departure from Ankara quickly reaffirmed that East-West détente had not relegated Turkey to the strategic sidelines.

In Athens, on the other hand, the mood immediately before the Iraqi occupation of Kuwait was one of some complacency. Greek officials shared the view expressed to us in Ankara that the collapse of the Warsaw Pact would weaken Turkey's claims on the United States and NATO for assistance and support. They saw this as an immense gain for Greece which, having just formed a conservative government under Constantine Mitsotakis, was thought to be well positioned to improve Greece's standing in Western capitals and to make the most of Turkey's anticipated strategic eclipse. This impression had been reinforced by Mitsotakis's warm reception in Washington less than two months after his election—the first visit of a Greek prime minister to the U.S. capital in twelve years. The Greeks, instead of being part of the neglected southeastern flank of NATO, were henceforth to be in the alliance's frontline facing the Middle East, where Greece's long Hellenistic and Orthodox involvement with the Arab world would uniquely qualify Athens to represent Western interests. The Persian Gulf crisis altered the Greek perspective as it did the Turkish. Once again, like it to not, their roles in support of Western policy were complementary. Turkey's wholehearted participation in the UN embargo of Iraq and its later support of allied military operations were indispensable, but Greek air space and naval support facilities in Crete were of signal importance in expediting military assistance from Western Europe to Saudi Arabia. It was a reminder that what geography had united, even the end of the Cold War could not put asunder.

"Hard cases make bad law" is the conventional wisdom of lawyers, and the Aegean is a hard case. Nearly 2,400 Greek islands, over 100 of them populated, are distributed across an irregularly shaped sea of about 80,000 square miles, which is smaller in surface area than the North American Great Lakes.[2] The Aegean is enclosed on the north and west by the Greek mainland and on the east by the Turkish mainland and is bounded, although not enclosed, on the south by Crete, the largest of the Greek islands (with a population of over 500,000) and the fifth largest in the Mediterranean. In the north, the Aegean's sole outlet is the straits of the Dardanelles, which lead to

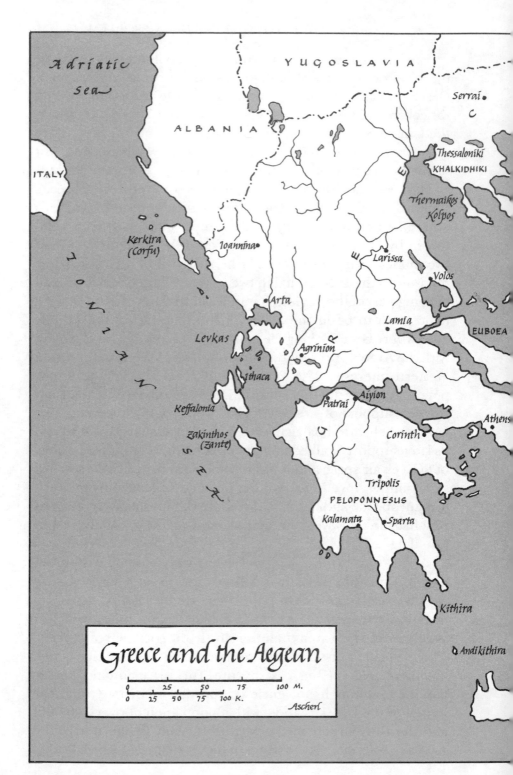

Greece and the Aegean

0 · · · 25 · · · 50 · · · 75 · · · 100 M.
0 · 25 · 50 · 75 · 100 K.

Ascherl

Adriatic
sea

YUGOSLAVIA

Serrai

ALBANIA

ITALY

Thessaloniki
KHALKIDHIKI

Thermaikos
Kolpos

Kerkira
(Corfu)

Ioannina

Larissa

Volos

Arta

Lamia

EUBOEA

Levkas

Agrinion

Ithaca

Aiyion

Keffalonia

Patrai

Athens

Zakinthos
(Zante)

Corinth

Tripolis

PELOPONNESUS

Kalamata

Sparta

Kithira

Andikithira

BULGARIA

Black Sea

Istanbul

Sea of Marmara

Kavalla

Alexandroupolis

Thasos

Samothraki

Imroz
(Gökçeada)

Canakkale

Bursa

Limnos

Tenedos
(Bozcaada)

Ayvalik

Lesvos

NORTHERN
SPORADHES

Skiros

AEGEAN

Psara

Khios

Izmir

Andros

ISLANDS

Samos

Aydin

Denizli

Makronisi

Tinos

Ikaria

Kea

Yioura

siros

Fournoi

Mikonos

Kithnos

Patmos

Serifos

Leros

Paros

Kalimnos

Sifnos

Naxos

Kos

Marmaris

Amorgos

Milos

Sikinos

Ios

Astipalaia

Nisiros

Simi

Thira

Tilos

Anafi

Khalki

Rhodes

Sea of Crete

Karpathos

Khania

Kasos

Iraklion

CRETE

the Sea of Marmara, and thence through the Bosphorus to the Black Sea. In the south, relatively narrow high-sea channels east and west of Crete and Rhodes connect the Aegean with the main body of the Mediterranean.

The Aegean dispute between Greece and Turkey concerns the territorial sea to which each country is entitled, delimitation of national air space, the extent to which the Greek islands must be demilitarized under existing treaties, and the rights of each state to explore and exploit whatever mineral resources may exist in the Aegean continental shelf. These central problems have given rise to others, such as the drawing of military command-and-control lines in the Aegean and the delineation of civil air flight information regions between Greece and Turkey. As we have seen, the failure to agree on command-and-control lines, like the withdrawal of Greece from NATO exercises in the Aegean, has weakened NATO's operational capability in an area where the interests of Europe, the Soviet Union, and the United States converge and where their access to the Middle East can be greatly facilitated or impeded. Beyond the boundaries of the Aegean, the Greek-Turkish confrontation not only has made the Cyprus problem infinitely more intractable but has aroused nationalist passions that aggravate other controversies like the status of the Moslem minority in Greek Thrace and of the Orthodox Church and its remaining congregation in Istanbul.

If we were to define the essential interests of Greece and Turkey in the Aegean and the policies needed to protect them in the future, we would certainly begin by noting that the geography of the region, so inconvenient from the standpoint of defense, navigation, and commercial development when Greece and Turkey are antagonistic, constitutes a formidable barrier to outside interference and a potentially profitable area for cooperation when they are not. The Aegean islands are what remain of a land bridge that, in the distant geologic past, linked the Greek and Turkish mainlands. Objectively regarded, Greek and Turkish interests would best be served not by interpreting them solely or even primarily in politico-military terms—as factors in a zero-sum game of national security—and consequently trying to fight the immutable geography of the region with diplomatic and military stratagems. In today's world, it would be more realistic to interpret these Aegean interests in politico-economic terms, as factors in a security environment changing too fundamentally to permit any power the luxury of "permanent friends or enemies," in Palmerston's words, or the convenience of plotting its position on an East-West grid.

It is, of course, easier to point out that the objective interests of Greece and Turkey argue in favor of their working together than to demonstrate how they can be persuaded to do so. Greece and Turkey are like veteran actors in a historical pageant, cast for centuries in antagonistic roles, now being called on to play mutually supporting parts in a completely new drama. They made the required costume change and became allies in 1952, although they were never comfortable with their new lines. Now the scene has changed again and they must undertake the process anew. Perhaps this time, with more latitude in interpreting their roles than they enjoyed during the Cold War, and more attention being paid by their allies, as it must be, to their special concerns, skillful diplomacy can produce a smoother performance. It should at least be possible to address the causes of Greek-Turkish problems, not simply the effects, and to do so in circumstances that allow NATO diplomats to look at the road ahead instead of remaining glued to their rear-view mirrors to see if the Soviets are gaining on them. It is very much in Western interests that the effort be made. The roles Turkey and Greece played in the Gulf crisis demonstrate that the original rationale for bringing them into NATO—their proximity to the Middle East—continues to be valid in a new strategic context.[3]

Any serious allied diplomatic initiative must begin by examining the main elements of Greek and Turkish bilateral differences in the Aegean, distinguishing between their vital and their tactical interests, estimating whether trade-offs are possible, and, if they are, how they can be negotiated.

The most basic, and at the same time, the most complicated of the Aegean issues is the shelf. The diplomatic history of the dispute is mainly a prolonged series of exchanges between Greece and Turkey about whether the shelf is more a problem in international law or in regional politics, whether, that is, it should be resolved by the International Court of Justice in the Hague or through bilateral negotiations. In February 1975, six months after the Cyprus crisis of the past summer had brought the two countries to the brink of war, a nonpolitical transition government in Ankara under Sadi Irmak agreed to join with Greece in making a joint appeal to the court. Almost immediately, Turkish political leaders, sensitive to the fact that existing legal precedent seemed to favor the Greek case, reversed this position and no joint submission was made. Finally, in August 1976, reacting to a Turkish attempt to survey the Aegean shelf in a disputed area west of the Greek island of Mytilini, Greece appealed unilaterally to the court for delimitation of the shelf and protection from Turkish efforts to explore it in the interim. A legal debate over the Greek application was conducted by Greece and Turkey until the court ruled in January 1979 that it lacked jurisdiction in the case. Should Greece and Turkey in the future reach agreement on the terms of a joint appeal, the case could be resubmitted. Meanwhile, in the absence of an agreed delineation of the shelf, attempts by one side to explore it in areas contested by the other have on several occasions nearly resulted in hostilities.[4]

Two commonsense observations can be made about the present status of the Aegean shelf. The first is that the shelf benefits neither party economically and is a political liability for both as long as it remains in dispute. The second is that Greece and Turkey have each, at one time or another, indicated their awareness that delineation of the shelf is both a legal and a political problem. Successive Turkish governments, although never returning to the position of the Irmak government in 1975, have accepted the competence of the International Court to rule on aspects of the case that the two parties are unable to resolve bilaterally and which would become, therefore, the basis for a joint submission to the court. Greece, for its part, agreed in the Bern Declaration of November 11, 1976[5] to engage in discussions with Turkey for the purpose of "educing certain principles and practical criteria which could be of use in the delimitation of the continental shelf between the two countries." Such discussions were held regularly at the level of secretaries general of the two Foreign Ministries until they were broken off by the Papandreou government after its election in October 1981. By most accounts, progress was made in narrowing differences on the issues involved. Even the Papandreou government, whose official position was that there was "nothing to negotiate" with the Turks, modified its stand after the March 1987 maritime crisis and resumed regular meetings with Ankara at the professional level.

Since Greece and Turkey have in the past agreed that the shelf dispute has both legal and political dimensions, a view that is also expressed by UN Security Council Resolution 395,[6] and since it is evident that their economic interests in the shelf will remain purely theoretical until they can explore and exploit its resources on the basis of a settlement, the underlying reason for the deadlock must be sought elsewhere, specifically in the fact that Greece and Turkey regard each other's positions on the Aegean shelf, like their differences on territorial sea limits, air space, and command-and-control lines, as aspects of the expansionist policies they charge each other with following. According to the Turks, "Greece does not seem to be content with what she has. She wishes to expand towards the east, at the expense of Turkey, first by turning the Aegean into a Greek sea and then by embarking upon even more ambitious projects to realize the so-called Megali Idea."[7] According to the Greeks, "the Aegean continental shelf (could) be demarcated and the matter would end just as it has done in similar disputes among other countries. . . . Turkey, on the contrary, [uses] the continental shelf question as an excuse or as a starting point for staking claims on Greek territory."[8]

The best way to unblock the shelf dispute, it would seem, is to address the territorial issue first, as we suggested earlier. Only then will Greece and Turkey feel free to discuss the proper weight that should be accorded legal and political factors in arriving at a solution that respects their individual interests in the subsea resources of the Aegean while recognizing their common interests. Only then can their Western allies be in a position to provide discreet assistance in getting to the substance of the dispute, especially if it is the alliance that has enabled Greece and

Turkey to dispose of the territorial issue by means of a NATO-guaranteed pact of nonaggression.

NATO might then approach the matter through the hitherto underutilized good offices of its secretary general in one of two ways: either by the secretary general himself offering to facilitate bilateral talks aimed at framing the terms of reference for a new submission to the International Court, or by proposing some form of nonjudicial arbitration, perhaps by a panel of Wise Men acceptable to Greece and Turkey and drawn from the ranks of elder statesmen in NATO countries. It ought not to be impossible to come up with a panel of arbiters whose eminence and impartiality enabled Athens and Ankara to accept their assistance without appearing to give anything away in advance. In both procedures, Greece would be able to point out that the case was being submitted to outside arbitration and Turkey that arbitration would be preceded by direct talks. Most important of all, when direct talks began they would be conducted out of the threatening shadow of the territorial issue.

If there were agreed procedures for arbitration of the shelf issue, air space and territorial sea problems would be easier to handle. Greece's insistence on its right to extend its territorial seas to twelve miles would, in particular, be affected because the Greek position relates as much to the shelf as to sea and air space above the shelf. These also have legal and political dimensions but, like Aegean command-and-control lines and the arming of the Greek islands, their military implications are of greater concern to Greece and Turkey, who have regarded them as key security issues since 1974. They, too, would look more negotiable if approached pragmatically and not as preliminary skirmishes in a battle over sovereignty. Stripped of chauvinistic embellishments, the question of how Greece and Turkey operate in the sea that geography invites them to share and history to dispute is no more impervious to diplomacy than the problems faced by Greece and Italy in the Ionian Sea or Australia and Papua New Guinea in the Torres Straits. The fact that Greece can derive comfort from the first case and Turkey from the second indicates that no Aegean settlement will spring from a single precedent or be successfully negotiated without taking into account both legal and political realities.

The vital interests of Greece and Turkey in Aegean sea and air spaces are definable and not necessarily incompatible. Greece needs uninterrupted political continuity between the Greek mainland and the islands, which are no less intrinsic to Greek sovereignty than Macedonia or the Peloponnesus. This means that no Greek government could accept an Aegean settlement that obliged Greek ships to traverse Turkish territorial waters while passing between the mainland and the islands. Nor could a Greek government accept military command-and-control arrangements in the Aegean that relinquished to Turkey primary responsibility for defense of the Greek islands against attack by a third party.[9]

Turkey, on the other hand, needs uninterrupted access to the high seas from the Turkish ports that stretch over 400 miles along the southwestern coast of Anatolia from Çanakkale at the southern end of the Turkish straits to Bodrum and Marmaris opposite the Greek islands of Kos and Rhodes. The most important Turkish port in this area is Izmir, which is both a major commercial shipping point and the headquarters for NATO's Commander of Allied Land Forces in Southeastern Europe (COMLANDSOUTHEAST). No Turkish government could accept a settlement of the territorial sea issue that severed the three high-sea corridors that link Turkey's southwestern ports—and also its main port, Istanbul, by way of the Sea of Marmara and the straits—to the Mediterranean.

Since both Greece and Turkey adhere in the Aegean to a six-mile territorial sea, which Turkey, in conformity with international practice, accepts as applying to the Greek islands, about 35 percent of the Aegean is presently Greek, 8.8 percent Turkish, and the remaining 56.2 percent is high seas. If Greece were to claim a twelve-mile territorial sea, in accordance with general provisions of the 1958 Law of the Sea Conference,[10] the Greek share of the Aegean would increase to 63.9 percent, the Turkish to 10 percent, and the Aegean high seas would be reduced to 26.1 percent.[11] In the latter case, no Turkish vessel could reach the high seas without passing through Greek territorial waters.

To emphasize the importance they attach to territorial sea issues, Greece and Turkey have taken equally uncompromising stands. Ankara has repeatedly stated that any action by Greece to extend its territorial sea from six to twelve miles would be a *casus* belli. Athens has reserved its right to extend to twelve miles, a position designed to protect its claims on the Aegean shelf, but has said it does not intend to do so. Greece has also made it clear that any attempt by Turkey to interfere with communications between the Greek mainland and the islands would result in immediate hostilities.

The issue of air space has similar strategic connotations but is complicated by the fact that Greece claims ten miles of air space around its islands, in contrast to its six-mile territorial sea, and because Greece and Turkey have been unable to agree on the delimitation of their Flight Information Regions (FIRs)—civil air traffic control zones which are drawn up with the agreement of member states by the International Civil Aviation Organization (ICAO).

It is international practice that a state's territorial seas and air space should be coterminous. Greece's position that its islands cannot be adequately defended with less than 10 miles of air space, given the speed of modern aircraft, creates a legal anomaly that not only Turkey but most other states, including the United States, have declined to accept. Greece points out that the ten-mile limit was established by Greek presidential decree in 1931 and was tacitly observed by Turkey (and presumably by other states) until 1974, when Ankara also withdrew its recognition of the boundaries of the Flight Information Region established by ICAO in 1952 and approved at that time by both Greece and Turkey. Ankara asserts that the 1952 decision, which made Athens the air traffic controller for flights virtually anywhere in the Aegean, imperils Turkish security in the atmosphere of mutual distrust that has existed since 1974. Ankara calls for a new, mid-Aegean FIR line and rejects Greek protests that the 1952 boundaries cannot be redrawn without the approval of Greece and ICAO. At the present time, the impasse over FIRs chiefly inconveniences air travelers between Ankara and Athens, who must now change planes in Istanbul, since direct flights across the Aegean were discontinued in 1974. As noted earlier, the ten miles of air space that Greece claims around its islands creates something more than an inconvenience. The danger of a tragedy by miscalculation in the Aegean skies is always present when foreign, especially Turkish, military aircraft challenge the Greek ten-mile limit and Greek air force interceptors are scrambled to shadow them. Such encounters have occurred on numerous occasions, especially during NATO or Turkish national military exercises. They have thus far resulted in nothing more serious than exchanges of diplomatic protests. However, the spectacle of one NATO ally conducting mock dogfights with another in aircraft supplied by a third does little to strengthen the alliance's credibility and much to emphasize NATO's responsibility to do more than it has to eliminate the risk of hostilities between two of its members.

In considering the negotiability of the territorial sea and air space issues, it is noteworthy that, although both Greece and Turkey qualify their acceptance of the Aegean status quo—Greece, by refusing to relinquish the right to extend its territorial sea to twelve miles, and Turkey, by refusing to accept the ten-mile limit claimed by Greece for its air space—the existing situation preserves, albeit precariously, the interests that both countries have called vital. Turkey has unimpeded access to the high seas and Greece has uninterrupted political continuity between the mainland and the islands. This is doubtless why Athens and Ankara have been willing to live for so long with a situation to which both profess to take serious exception.

They have also lived for this length of time with their differences over Aegean military issues—command-and-control lines, fortification of the Greek islands, creation of the Turkish Aegean Army, and future establishment of a NATO command in Larissa. As we have seen, these problems, unlike the political disputes of Greece and Turkey, have been impossible for the alliance to ignore. We also saw that the valiant efforts of NATO military commanders to cobble together purely military solutions that would enable the alliance to conduct business as usual on its southeastern flank have been doomed to failure as long as the underlying political causes remained unresolved.[12] Turkey is correct in arguing that conditions that prevailed when ICAO drew FIR lines in 1952 have changed. Greece is justified in making the same point about the demilitarization of the Greek islands decreed by the treaties of Lausanne and Paris in 1923 and 1947, respectively.[13] Until the legal framework within which Greek-Turkish relations are conducted is brought up to date, the prospect of finding lasting solutions to any of their problems is dim. But the prospect of finding a new legal framework is itself remote until enough mutual confidence is restored to negotiate one. At present, nothing is negotiable because each side imputes expansionist motives to the other and the allies of both decline to become involved. This diplomatic dead end serves the interests of no one—not Greece or Turkey or NATO—but everyone claims to be powerless to alter it. Greece and Turkey hold firm to positions on the shelf that effectively preclude the exploitation of its resources by either; they assert rights in Aegean seas and air space that they cannot oblige the other to recognize without hostilities that would be disastrous to both; and they deploy their military forces as though such hostilities were feasible instruments of national policy.

In this sorry situation there are a few positive elements. Of these, perhaps the most significant is that Greece and Turkey have repeatedly shown by their prudent handling of past Aegean crises that they do not really want hostilities. Their words rather than their actions have been intransigent. Strong language on national issues reduces domestic political risks in all countries, and the most audible Greek and Turkish voices— government leaders and the press—are most sensitive to such risks. Others, including prominent Greek and Turkish business-men, cultural leaders, and a few courageous and independent-minded politicians and journalists, have shown that support exists in both countries for improving bilateral relations. It is the diplomatic process of reconciliation that is stalled and needs to be jump started. The logical vehicle to accomplish this would be NATO, acting with the active encouragement of the United States.

Admittedly, more will be needed than a jolt of energy from outside. An important element will be clearheaded and self-confident political leadership in Athens and Ankara of the kind supplied in 1930 by Venizelos and Ataturk. This has sometimes existed in the years since World War II but not often at the same time in both capitals. The strong Karamanlis government that ruled Greece for five years after the fall of the Colonels in 1974 dealt in Ankara with weak Turkish coalition governments. When Gen. Kenan Evren imposed military rule on the hopelessly divided Turkish politicians in 1980 and, in a gesture of good will to Athens, agreed to Greek reintegration into the NATO military structure, Greece was entering a pre-electoral period with a new, politically weak prime minister, George Rallis. By the time the succeeding Papandreou government began to take its relations with Turkey seriously in 1987, the Turkish political situation was again in flux, and Papandreou himself had been weakened by accumulating internal problems. Diplomacy, however, cannot await the appearance of ideal leaders operating in the most propitious of political climates. It must work with conditions as they are. The objective reasons for negotiating Greek-Turkish differences are undeniable. The rewards for both countries in terms of enhanced national security and enriched economic prospects in the Aegean are clear. By assuming some of the political risks of negotiation that have intimidated Greek and Turkish leaders, NATO not only can jump start the negotiating process but help steer it to a successful conclusion.

Once negotiations that address problems on their merits and not as maneuvers in a larger contest to control the Aegean have begun, a series of trade-offs will become available that would have the diplomatically rare and desirable consequence of leaving both parties better off than they were before. On the territorial seas issue, for example, Greece reserves a right it does not intend to exercise and Turkey a threat it does not intend to carry out. In circumstances in which the ghosts of presumed expansionism had been exorcized, nothing would be more logical and less costly than for Greece formally to renounce any intention to extend its territorial seas to twelve miles in exchange for Turkey's agreement to negotiate a pact of nonaggression, coupled, perhaps, with its renewed acceptance of the ten miles of airspace that Greece claims around its Aegean islands. Equally beneficial to the interests of both would be agreement by Turkey to redeploy or demobilize the so-called Army of the Aegean (which puts Turkish forces where they are not needed) in exchange for Greek demilitarization of the Dodecanese (which puts Greek forces where they are hard to defend). In a restored atmosphere of mutual trust it would then make sense for Turkey to acquiesce in Greek fortification of the island of Limnos, where Greece's legal case is exceedingly strong and the enhanced military capability of a trusted ally would contribute far more than demilitarization to the defense of the Turkish straits. In return, Greece would cease objecting to the emplacement of NATO-supplied missiles along the Anatolian approaches to the Dardanelles where, in the happier state of Greek-Turkish relations then prevailing, they could be employed to defend not only the straits but the islands of the north Aegean from attack by a third party. These actions would, in turn, free Greece and Turkey from the need to regard secondary disputes, like that over the boundaries of the Aegean Flight Information Region, as tests of sovereignty affecting their primary interests. Available evidence suggests that Greek and Turkish representatives have in the past come close to agreement on the FIR dispute which, as long as it remains unresolved, damages not only their bilateral relations but the revenue they earn from Aegean tourism.

Success in these undertakings would greatly simplify the drawing of Aegean command-and-control lines, creation of the Seventh Allied Tactical Air Force Headquarters in Larissa, and other problems left over from Greece's still incomplete reintegration into the military structure of NATO. After the root political causes of the Aegean confrontation—national distrust and insecurity—were relieved, the military symptoms that have so aggravated NATO since 1974—skewed Aegean exercises, footnotes and circumlocutions in NATO communiqués, vetoed country chapters and aid allocations, to recall a few—would more readily yield to the restorative diplomacy of CINCEUR and his subordinate commanders. In whichever direction NATO needed to face, it would once again have a southeastern flank it could rely upon.

10

FROM DOCTRINE TO DIPLOMACY

The speed and decisiveness with which Iraq was forced to withdraw from Kuwait by a U.S.–led military campaign, endorsed by virtually all members of the United Nations, has caused Greeks and Greek Cypriots to ask plaintively why Turkish forces have been permitted to remain in northern Cyprus since July 1974. The answer for most of the rest of the world is that Saddam Hussein's motives, whatever they were when he invaded Kuwait in August 1990, did not include protecting an embattled Iraqi minority. Nor was Kuwait the subject of a treaty of guarantee, like Cyprus, or the object of an attempted coup d'état, like that engineered by the Greek Colonels against President Makarios. Not to mention that Turkey did not announce its intention to obliterate the Republic of Cyprus from the map or turn it into an Anatolian province.

But if the circumstances of the two cases are different, the principle involved is not. The Republic of Cyprus is today, following the restoration of Kuwaiti sovereignty, the only member-state of the United Nations with foreign forces remaining on its soil against the will of its government.[1] Even the departure of Vietnamese forces from Cambodia seems more likely than the departure of Turkish troops from Cyprus. And until this occurs, or until conditions are created in which a smaller Turkish security force can remain with the consent of the Cypriot government, Cyprus will continue to be a tinderbox.

When the tinderbox ignites, as we should have learned from past experience, Greece and Turkey will be the first to feel the heat, but the United States will be first in the bucket brigade. This in itself should cause Washington to pay more attention to fire prevention in the region than it has in the past. Many approaches to the interrelated problems of Cyprus and the Aegean are possible. Several have been suggested in this study, which inclines to the view that the UN secretary general's inter-

145

communal talks, worthwhile as they are in keeping communications open between Greek and Turkish Cypriots, are unlikely to produce a lasting settlement because they approach the problem from the wrong end. In the view of the author, disentangling the problem of Cyprus will require also, and probably first, disentangling the problems of Greece and Turkey. The advice of Ariadne to Theseus was to find his way out of the labyrinth by starting at the beginning.

Accepting this thesis is not, however, a prerequisite for a new diplomatic effort to improve the situation in both Cyprus and the Aegean. The secretary general's talks have been going on since 1968 and, in the absence of a new round of fighting or the withdrawal of the UN peacekeeping force,[2] can go on indefinitely into the future. They need not defer to a separate diplomatic initiative aimed at creating greater mutual confidence between Athens and Ankara by means of a treaty of friendship and nonaggression, and subsequently at jump starting serious Greek-Turkish negotiations on their Aegean problems, under acceptable international auspices. On the contrary, the purpose of a separate diplomatic initiative would be to facilitate the secretary general's task, not to replace it.

There is little doubt that if such an initiative is to be taken, the United States will have to be behind it, not necessarily as the chief actor—indeed, as we have seen, there are important reasons why both Greece and Turkey would have reservations about an overly conspicuous U.S. role—but certainly as the chief instigator. The Western Europeans have been notably reluctant to be drawn into the web of Greek-Turkish differences, and only the British, by virtue of their role as a guarantor power, have been unable to escape involvement in the Cyprus problem. This is not to say, however, that the Europeans are blind to the advantages of a Greek-Turkish settlement. In the councils of the EC, the CFE, and the CSCE, among others, they have had ample opportunity to see how the unresolved problems of Greece and Turkey can interfere with the conduct of other business. The Germans, the French, the Dutch, and the Italians, as well as the British, all have special familiarity with conflicting Greek and Turkish policies and with the internal political factors influencing policymakers in Athens and Ankara. Once they were convinced that the United States was committed to working quietly with the Greeks and Turks (and with the Western Europeans themselves) to begin negotiations—first leading to a nonaggression pact, later to resolution of the Aegean shelf and other bilateral issues—there is every reason to believe that the Europeans would be willing to play a constructive role, whether it involved démarches by their governments to get the process started or the selection of Wise Men qualified to assist the Greeks and Turks themselves on the issues. The diplomatic mechanism to be employed—NATO, the EC, or CSCE—may be subject to discussion, but it is clear that a serious effort will require active promotion by the United States if it is to be undertaken and European participation if it is to be successful.

Regarding the appropriate diplomatic mechanism, the advantages offered by NATO are fairly clear: Both Greece and Turkey are members, and the organization has the experience and leverage lacking in other bodies. Neither Greece nor Turkey believes NATO has been impartial about their disputes in the past—Greece, in particular, nourishes deep-seated grievances about the alliance's inaction in 1974—but if the institutional role for NATO is primarily to guarantee a Greek-Turkish nonaggression pact, something of greater interest in Athens than in Ankara, these subjective perceptions of the alliance's past record, and the reasons for it, are not of central importance. Cyprus is not, of course, a member of NATO, but the contribution of the alliance to an intercommunal settlement, by assisting in the improvement of Greek-Turkish relations, would be purely indirect. The intercommunal talks under UN auspices would not be interrupted, and the nonaligned status of Cyprus would not be compromised.

Some observers believe that CSCE offers a better forum than NATO for the Greeks, Turks, and Cypriots, all of whom are members and all of whom participated in the meetings in Valletta at the beginning of 1991 that resulted in the adoption of the "Provisions for a CSCE Procedure for Peaceful Settlement of Disputes." While it is fervently to be hoped that the mechanism proposed in Valletta will eventually become a useful instrument

in the peace process, there is room for skepticism that it is yet
appropriate for use in the Aegean or Cyprus disputes. For one
thing, the Greeks and Turks hotly debated the wording of Section XII and formally expressed different interpretations of its
scope.[3] Beyond this obstacle to the application of the CSCE
mechanism is the more general objection that an untested procedure with little institutional weight behind it or experience to
draw on would be of limited utility in resolving problems as
complicated and entrenched as those of Greece, Turkey, and
Cyprus.

The EC itself may one day be equipped to perform functions of conflict resolution among its members, but that day has
certainly not arrived. Reflecting on the failure of the EC to adopt
a common European policy in the gulf crisis, the president of the
European Commission, Jacques Delors, said in March 1991, "On
foreign policy, the current situation cannot continue. This has
been made abundantly clear by the Gulf Crisis. We see it every
day in the absence of common and global thinking on matters
affecting the Community's external relations."[4] Obviously, much
work remains to be done before the EC has the internal political
unity and sense of shared political purpose that will allow it to
take on conflict resolution assignments as difficult as the ones
under discussion. Even if the EC were better equipped than it is,
the fact that Greece is a member and Turkey is not would seem
automatically to disqualify the EC from serving as mediator of
the conflict or guarantor of a settlement ending it.

NATO, alone among the international organizations in
which Greece and Turkey are both represented, possesses the
incentive, the experience, and the clout to make a difference if it
chooses to do so.

Here arises the question of "ripeness." With or without help,
are the Greeks, the Turks, and the Cypriots ready to resolve their
problems? No third party or collective mechanism can relieve
them of the ultimate responsibility to negotiate satisfactory settlements of their own disputes and to abide by them. There are
qualified American and European observers who believe the
time is not "ripe" for a settlement.[5] The difficulty with the
ripeness argument is that it amounts to a self-fulfilling prophecy.

If a diplomatic initiative fails to solve a given problem in international relations, the problem was not ripe. If it succeeds, it was. In fact, the nature of international relations is less horticultural than kinetic. When a diplomatic problem becomes ripe, it does not necessarily fall from the tree. Sometimes it explodes. It is the purpose of diplomacy to take international problems before they are ripe and to defuse them before they explode.

With the glowing exception of U.S. diplomacy immediately after World War II, the period of the Truman Doctrine and the Marshall Plan, this is not a skill that U.S. foreign policy has cultivated with any particular distinction. For reasons noted earlier, we are better at handling crises than conditions, and our approach to international relations is incremental rather than continuous. We seem suspicious, contemptuous even, of diplomacy as a method of conducting foreign affairs, perhaps viewing it as an outmoded European way of doing business that is unsuited to the new world order that is always just around the corner. We can hope that will change. During the Civil War, too many generals in command of key sectors were untrained, or inadequately trained, political appointees, and the resulting slaughter taught us the value of a professional corps of senior officers. The United States would need to undertake fewer military interventions abroad if it used its diplomatic forces as effectively as it does its military forces.

The question also arises why a U.S. administration would wish at this time to promote a diplomatic initiative that will be hard to get off the ground and even harder to steer safely to its destination. Here the answer must be that all signs indicate that Greece, Turkey, and Cyprus are going to be more important allies and friends of the United States in the future than at any time since President Truman warned, in March 1947, that "Should we fail to aid Greece and Turkey . . . the effect will be far reaching to the West as well as the East."[6] As the gulf crisis demonstrated, the United States needs reliable access routes to the Middle East. The best routes lead through Greece, Turkey, and Cyprus. How we are able to restructure our military commands in the region; how NATO is able to relate to threats that, in the liturgy of the alliance, are "out-of-area" but which, in the real world, affect the vital interests of all NATO members; how the United States and its European allies are able to keep informed of military developments affecting the regional balance of forces—all these things will become easier or more difficult in direct proportion to the strength of our relationships with Greece, Turkey, and Cyprus and in indirect proportion to the strength of their relationships with each other. If the Turkish role is bound to be indispensable in linking the United States and Western Europe with the Middle East, the role of Greece will be equally so with regard to the Balkans. The exhilaration felt by Eastern Europeans when they were released from the constraints of Soviet domination has given way to ethnic ferment and frustration. The "new order" in Eastern Europe is as unclear and the situation as explosive as it is in the Middle East. The United States and NATO will need, at minimum, to follow developments closely, and Greece will continue to be an essential access point, as well as a state whose historic ties with the region, including its cultural and religious ties, can prove influential if instability worsens.

The case of Greece, Turkey, and Cyprus is, for these reasons, a good place for the United States to begin anticipating problems before they require armed rather than diplomatic intervention. Greece and Turkey are long-standing allies of the United States, and Cyprus is a small, friendly state that has extended significant assistance to us in perilous times. All three are heavily burdened by defense budgets that can no longer be rationalized in Cold War terms. Not only is the arms race between Greece and Turkey accelerating—with both competing for large quantities of semi-obsolescent conventional U.S. weapons that are becoming available as we scale down the level of NATO armaments in Western Europe—but an arms race is beginning in Cyprus, where, in the absence of a political settlement, the Republic of Cyprus is making heavy investments in new weaponry, especially French,[7] the cost of which will aggravate a budget squeeze already intensified by reduced revenues from tourism after the gulf war.

The U.S. government in these circumstances should spend less time trying to eliminate or circumvent the 7:10 ratio and more time working to reduce the overall level of armaments in the area. We should certainly not contribute to the existing arms race, whether for reasons of "gratitude" to our allies in the gulf war, or because others may step in as prime suppliers of military hardware if we decline to escalate our deliveries. Further, to burden impoverished countries that are already spending 7 to 10 percent of GDP on their military budgets is to behave like an irresponsible friend. The result can only be to worsen their relations, put a sharper cutting edge on their differences, and impede their prospects for economic recovery.

The most critical problems confronting Greece and Turkey today, and for a long time to come, are certain to be economic. Greece has been obliged to seek a $3 billion loan from its EC partners on terms severe enough to make the International Monetary Fund look like Santa Claus. The disbursement of three tranches of EC assistance will depend on Greece's reaching specific economic goals by specific dates. These include sharply phased reductions in the rate of inflation and the public sector deficit, both politically difficult for any Greek government to achieve without significant reductions in defense spending. Greece, in addition, is faced by a potentially serious refugee problem. The influx of Albanian refugees, most of them ethnically Greek, caused by recent political tremors in Albania, worried the Greek government enough for Prime Minister Mitsotakis, after a flying visit to Tirana, to appeal publicly to the refugees to return to Albania. The threatened breakup of Yugoslavia, and the political and economic instability elsewhere in Eastern Europe—not excluding the Soviet Union, where an estimated 325,000 ethnic Greeks remain[8]—can only narrow Greece's economic margins. Meanwhile, Turkey, whose problems, like those of Greece, are a legacy of decades of inefficient state intervention in the economy compounded by excessive defense spending, is looking for astronomic amounts of military and economic aid in compensation for losses of revenue from the gulf war. Even if foreign aid to Turkey approaches the sums sought, which is unlikely, a new Turkish military buildup, aiming, for example, to double coproduction of F-16s to reach a total of 320 aircraft, seems ill-suited to Turkey's economic and strategic needs. Turks admittedly live in a dangerous neighborhood, but the threat today is one of regional instability and ethnic violence, not superpower aggression. The abortive Kurdish revolt against Saddam Hussein in northern Iraq has not only saddled Turkey with a difficult refugee problem but made it politically essential for Ankara to press ahead with economic development in the southeast if Turkey's own Kurdish problem is not to boil over. In the radically restructured world inhabited by Turkey today, economic vulnerabilities are likely to be more dangerous than military ones.

This is true for all of us, not least the United States, and it is another sound reason to rethink the rationale underlying our relations. Armed confrontation in the Aegean and in Cyprus preserves at great expense a situation that is unstable and inherently damaging to the long-term interests of Greece, Turkey, and Cyprus alike. All three are locked into tactical positions that effectively block their road to the future by putting at risk their prospects for economic growth, political stability, and territorial security at minimum cost. The paradox of their entanglement is that each pursues a prized objective that cannot be attained unless the others attain theirs: Turkey's interest in eventual membership in the European Community would best be served by removing Turkish troops from Cyprus; Greece's interest in strengthening its security in the Aegean would best be served by supporting Turkish membership in the EC; and the Republic of Cyprus's interest in preventing the permanent partition of the island would best be served by lifting the economic embargo imposed on the north. The interests of the United States would best be served if all three of these things happened.

They can and, with a more skillful diplomatic touch and more sustained attention than we have devoted to their problems in the past, we can help Greece, Turkey, and Cyprus begin the process of accommodation. U.S. governments, which are not taken seriously at home unless they have a "doctrine," like to codify foreign policy and can become disoriented when other states—adversaries or friends—appear to deviate from agreed codes of conduct. The relations of the United States with Greece and Turkey, and by extension with Cyprus were codified in 1947 by the Truman Doctrine, which was an expression of our policy toward the Soviet Union, not a blueprint for our relations with each other. The end of the Cold War enables us to establish a new foundation for our relationship, one that is better informed by history and better adapted to the priorities of a changing strategic terrain.

APPENDIX A

Letter from U.S. Secretary of State Dulles to Greek Prime Minister Papagos, September 18, 1955*

I have followed with concern the dangerous deterioration of Greek-Turkish relations caused by the Cyprus question. Regardless of the causes of this disagreement, which are complex and numerous, I believe that the unity of the North Atlantic community, which is the basis of our common security, must be restored without delay.

Since the time, almost a decade ago, when Communist expansion first posed a serious threat to the free world, the close and friendly cooperation of Greece and Turkey has proved a powerful deterrent to Communist ambitions in the eastern Mediterranean. In Korea, Greek and Turkish troops fought valiantly, side by side, to repel the Communist aggressors.

I cannot believe that in the face of this record of common achievement, any problem will long disrupt the course of Greek-Turkish friendship. Nor can I believe that the unhappy events of the past two weeks will reverse policies of cooperation which were initiated twenty-five years ago under the far-sighted leadership of Eleftherios Venizelos and Kemal Ataturk.

Since 1947 the United States has made very considerable efforts to assist Greece and Turkey to maintain their freedom and to achieve greater social and economic progress. We have extended this assistance—and extend it now—because we be-

* Text reprinted from Paul E. Zinner, ed., *Documents on American Foreign Relations: 1955* (New York: Council on Foreign Relations, 1956), p. 167. The text of the letter from the secretary of state to the prime minister of Turkey (Menderes) is identical to this letter, except that the two countries are named in reverse order.

lieve that the partnership of Greece and Turkey constitutes a strong bulwark of the free world in a critical area.

If that bulwark should be materially weakened, the consequences could be grave indeed. I urge you therefore to make every effort to assure that the effectiveness of your partnership is not impaired by present disagreements.

I am confident that the spirit of close cooperation that Greece and Turkey have so often demonstrated in the past as fellow members of the United Nations, the North Atlantic Treaty Organization and the Balkan Alliance will enable you to transcend immediate differences in the interests of free world unity.

APPENDIX B

Letter from President Johnson
to Turkish Prime Minister Inönü,
June 5, 1964[*]

Dear Mr. Prime Minister,

I am gravely concerned by the information which I have had through Ambassador Hare from you and your Foreign Minister that the Turkish Government is contemplating a decision to intervene by military force to occupy a portion of Cyprus. I wish to emphasize, in the fullest friendship and frankness, that I do not consider that such a course of action by Turkey, fraught with such far reaching consequences, is consistent with the commitment of your government to consult fully in advance with the United States. Ambassador Hare has indicated that you postponed your decision for a few hours in order to obtain my views. I put to you personally whether you really believe that it is appropriate for your government, in effect, to present an ultimatum to an ally who has demonstrated such staunch support over the years as has the United States for Turkey. I must, therefore, first urge you to accept the responsibility for complete consultation with the United States before any such action is taken.

It is my impression that you believe that such intervention by Turkey is permissible under the provisions of the Treaty of Guarantee of 1960. I must call your attention, however, to our understanding that the proposed intervention by Turkey would be for the purpose of supporting an attempt by Turkish Cypriot leaders to partition the island, a solution which is specifically excluded by the Treaty of Guarantee. Further, that treaty re-

* Text reprinted from Glafkos Clerides, *Cyprus: My Deposition*, vol. 2 (Nicosia: Alithia Publishing, 1989), pp. 115–118.

quires consultation among the guarantor powers. It is the view of the United States that the possibilities of such consultation have by no means been exhausted in this situation and that, therefore, the reservation of the right to take unilateral action is not yet applicable.

I must call to your attention also, Mr. Prime Minister, the obligations of NATO. There can be no question in your mind that a Turkish intervention in Cyprus would lead to a military engagement between Turkish and Greek forces. Secretary of State Rusk declared at a recent meeting of the ministerial council of NATO in The Hague that war between Turkey and Greece must be considered as "literally unthinkable." Adhesion to NATO, in its very essence, means that NATO countries will not wage war on each other. Germany and France have buried centuries of animosity and hostility in becoming NATO allies; nothing less can be expected from Greece and Turkey. Furthermore, a military intervention in Cyprus by Turkey could lead to direct involvement by the Soviet Union. I hope you will understand that your NATO allies have not had a chance to consider whether they have an obligation to protect Turkey against the Soviet Union if Turkey takes a step which results in Soviet intervention without the full consent and understanding of its NATO allies.

Further, Mr. Prime Minister, I am concerned about the obligations of Turkey as a member of the United Nations. The United Nations has provided forces on the island to keep the peace. Their task has been difficult but, during the past several weeks, they have been progressively successful in reducing the incidents of violence on that island. The United Nations Mediator has not yet completed his work. I have no doubt that the general membership of the United Nations would react in the strongest terms to unilateral action by Turkey which would defy the efforts of the United Nations and destroy any prospect that the United Nations could assist in obtaining a reasonable and peaceful settlement of this difficult problem.

I wish also, Mr. Prime Minister, to call your attention to the bilateral agreement between the United States and Turkey in the field of military assistance. Under Article IV of the agreement with Turkey of July 1947, your government is required to obtain

United states consent for the use of military assistance for purposes other than those for which such assistance was furnished. Your government has on several occasions acknowledged to the United States that you fully understand this condition. I must tell you in all candor that the United States cannot agree to the use of any United States supplied military equipment for a Turkish intervention in Cyprus under present circumstances.

Moving to the practical results of the contemplated Turkish move, I feel obligated to call to your attention in the most friendly fashion the fact that such a Turkish move could lead to the slaughter of tens of thousands of Turkish Cypriots on the island of Cyprus. Such an action on your part would unleash the furies and there is no way by which military action on your part could be sufficiently effective to prevent wholesale destruction of many of those whom you are trying to protect. The presence of United Nations forces could not prevent such a catastrophe.

You may consider that what I have said is much too severe and that we are disregardful of Turkish interests in the Cyprus situation. I should like to assure you that this is not the case. We have exerted ourselves both publicly and privately to assure the safety of Turkish Cypriots and to insist that a final solution of the Cyprus problem should rest upon the consent of the parties most directly concerned. It is possible that you feel in Ankara that the United States has not been sufficiently active in your behalf. But surely you know that our policy has caused the liveliest resentment in Athens (where demonstrations have been aimed against us) and has led to a basic alienation between the United States and Archbishop Makarios. As I said to your Foreign Minister in our conversation just a few weeks ago, we value very highly our relations with Turkey. We have considered you as a great ally with fundamental common interests. Your security and prosperity have been a deep concern of the American people and we have expressed that concern in the most practical terms. You and we have fought together to resist the ambitions of the communist world revolution. This solidarity has meant a great deal to us and I would hope that it means a great deal to your government and to your people. We have no intention of lending any support to any solution of Cyprus which endangers the Turkish Cypriot community. We have not been able to find a final solution because this is, admittedly, one of the most complex problems on earth. But I wish to assure you that we have been deeply concerned about the interests of Turkey and of the Turkish Cypriots and will remain so.

Finally, Mr. Prime Minister, I must tell you that you have posed the gravest issues of war and peace. These are issues which go far beyond the bilateral relations between Turkey and the United States. They not only will certainly involve war between Turkey and Greece but could involve wider hostilities because of the unpredictable consequences which a unilateral intervention in Cyprus could produce. You have your responsibilities as chief of the government of Turkey; I also have mine as President of the United States. I must, therefore, inform you in the deepest friendship that unless I can have your assurance that you will not take such action without further and fullest consultation I cannot accept your injunction to Ambassador Hare of secrecy and must immediately ask for emergency meetings of the NATO Council and of the United Nations Security Council.

I wish it were possible for us to have a personal discussion of this situation. Unfortunately, because of the special circumstances of our present constitutional position, I am not able to leave the United States. If you could come here for a full discussion I would welcome it. I do feel that you and I carry a very heavy responsibility for the general peace and for the possibilities of a sane and peaceful resolution of the Cyprus problem. I ask you, therefore, to delay any decisions which you and your colleagues might have in mind until you and I have had the fullest and frankest consultation.

Sincerely,

LYNDON B. JOHNSON

APPENDIX C

Letter from U.S. Secretary of State
Henry Kissinger
to Greek Foreign Minister Dimitri Bitsios,
April 10, 1976*

Dear Mr Minister,

Thank you for your letter of April 7th, in which you posed some questions regarding United States policy in the Eastern Mediterranean. I welcome this opportunity to make our position clear with regard to these issues.

You have asked about our attitude toward the resolution of disputes in the Eastern Mediterranean and particularly in the Aegean area. In this regard I should like to reiterate our conviction that these disputes must be settled through peaceful procedures and that each side should avoid provocative actions. We have previously stated our belief that neither side should seek a military solution to these disputes. This remains United States policy. Therefore the United States would actively and unequivocally oppose either side's seeking a military solution and will make a major effort to prevent such a course of action.

I should like to reemphasize, with regard to Cyprus, that the United States remains fully committed to the objective of an early and just settlement of this issue. As I said in my United Nations address, the present dividing lines in Cyprus cannot be permanent. There must be just territorial arrangements.

We intend to contribute actively in the search for a solution to the Cyprus problem that will preserve the independence, sovereignty and territorial integrity of Cyprus.

With regard to the defense relationship between Greece and the United States, I believe it would be useful if you could come

* Text reprinted from Dimitri Bitsios, *Pera Ăpo Ta Synora* (Beyond the Borders) (Athens: Estia, 1982), pp. 253–54.

to Washington to discuss this issue in detail. I would welcome an opportunity to discuss with you other subjects of mutual interest as well. At that time we could agree on the framework of a new Defense Cooperation Agreement between the United States and Greece that would benefit both of our countries and contribute to the maintenance of peace and security in the Eastern Mediterranean.

Warm regards,

H. KISSINGER

APPENDIX D

Mutual Defense Cooperation Agreement of May 30, 1990, Between the Government of the United States of America and the Government of the Hellenic Republic*

Preamble

As an expression of their common desire for an improved defense relationship, the government of the United States and the government of the Hellenic Republic are entering into a new defense cooperation agreement guided by the following principles:

The United States and Greece reaffirm their commitment to the purposes and principles of the United Nations Charter, and, in this context, to the exercise of their inherent right of individual and collective self-defense recognized in Article 51 of the Charter;

The United States and Greece reaffirm that their relations and cooperation are based on a common devotion to the principles of freedom, democracy, human rights, justice and social progress;

The United States and Greece confirm their recognition of the fact that their cooperation in the field of defense, as in all other fields, is based on the principles of mutual benefit and full respect for the sovereign equality, independence and interests of the two countries;

The United States and Greece reaffirm their respect for international law including existing treaties of particular relevance to the region, and their resolve to act in accordance with treaties a well as bilateral and multilateral arrangements to which

* Text reprinted from *Greece's Weekly* (Athens), July 16, 1990, p. 134.

they are both party, including the North Atlantic Treaty and the Helsinki Final Act;

The United States and Greece declare their dedication to the maintenance of peace and their commitment to respect the principle of refraining from actions threatening to peace; reiterate their firm determination mutually to safeguard and protect the security, sovereignty, independence and territorial integrity of their respective countries against actions threatening to peace, including armed attack or threat thereof; and confirm their resolve to oppose actively and unequivocally any such attempt or action and their commitment to make appropriate major efforts to prevent such a course of action;

The United States and Greece reaffirm their dedication to the principle that international disputes shall be settled through peaceful means; and their continuing firm resolve to contribute actively to the early and just settlement of existing international disputes in the region which particularly concern either Party to this Agreement through peaceful means that accord with the purposes and principles of the United Nations Charter;

The United States and Greece affirm that this Agreement is compatible with their respective constitutions and other laws, their common defense interests and undertakings, their respective national interests and sovereign rights; and that furthermore nothing in this Agreement is intended to harm the relations of either Party with any third country.

NOTES

INTRODUCTION

1. *Europe's New Pilgrims: A Voyage of Freedom,* President Bush's Thanksgiving Day address to the nation, November 22, 1989 (Washington, D.C.: Department of State, Bureau of Public Affairs, Current Policy 1229).

CHAPTER 1

1. CENTO was envisaged by the United States and Britain as an alliance that would block Soviet access to the Middle East and South Asia. Turkey represented the key link between CENTO and NATO, since it was the only state to be a member of both treaty organizations. The center of CENTO collapsed in 1958 with the overthrow of the conservative, Western-oriented Iraqi monarchy by military officers who introduced a policy of nonalignment and withdrew Iraq from CENTO in 1959. The United States had observer status in CENTO but, in deference to Israel, with which Iraq was still formally at war, it did not seek full membership.
2. Iran's political spasms have dominated the NEA assistant secretary's attention, and that of his superiors, on many subsequent occasions, but, since 1974, not at the expense of Greece and Turkey, which were finally transferred that year into the Bureau of European Affairs.
3. Which, like the Clifford mission the year before, appears, at least in part, to have been motivated by the Carter administration's desire to achieve enough progress in Cyprus to justify substantial Turkish troop withdrawals and the lifting of the congressionally imposed arms embargo on Turkey.
4. Here again, the Nimetz proposals are an exception. The State Department counselor's hand was strengthened by the fact that Secretary of State Vance had gained direct experience in the area from his 1967 mission. The proposals probably failed because they were seen by the Greek side as the prelude to a new effort by the Carter administration to lift the Turkish arms embargo.
5. Vance Report. Quotation from notes in author's files.
6. Excerpt from the State Department's instructions to Vance, November 22, 1967. Author's notes.
7. The same systemic propensities, it should be noted, also impede the development of long-range policies in vitally important areas like energy conservation and environmental pollution. Policymakers are likely to see these as no-win situations, with a politically dangerous cutting edge. Career officials at the working level are left to carve out small pieces of the action, leaving the larger problem unaffected.

8. Henry A. Kissinger, *The Troubled Partnership* (New York, McGraw-Hill, 1965), p. 93.
9. Before the 1990–1991 gulf crisis, there were an estimated 7,000 U.S. military personnel in Turkey and 3,700 in Greece.
10. In 1958 Greek trade with the United States, as a percentage of its total trade, was 13.6 percent for imports and 13.7 percent for exports. Turkey's was 19.5 percent and 27.8 percent, respectively. In 1986, the respective figures were 8.7 percent and 4.2 percent for Greece and 4.4 percent and 9.2 percent for Turkey. This decline has continued. In 1990, for example, two-way trade between the United States and Greece was only $1,271,500,000 and with Turkey only $3,433,500,000. These figures reflect a trade relationship comparable to that with a small state like Haiti, which has a population of slightly over five million inhabitants and has received U.S. aid that amounts to a particle of that given to Greece and Turkey (Department of Commerce statistics).
11. The text of the U.S.–Turkish DECA is in *U.S. Military Installations in NATO's Southern Region,* Report to House Subcommittee on Europe and the Middle East by Congressional Research Service, October 7, 1986, p. 347.
12. The Papandreou government's fear was that any reference to NATO in the agreement might imply that the joint facilities would continue to exist as long as Greece remained a member of the alliance.
13. The text of the U.S.-Turkish DECA is in *U.S. Military Installations in NATO's Southern Region,* Report to House Subcommittee on Europe and the Middle East by Congressional Research Service, October 7, 1986, p. 329. It must be added that the laconic style of the 1983 preamble disappeared when the Defense and Economic Cooperation Agreement was renegotiated in 1990 with a more conservative Greek government. The preamble to the 1990 DECA is replete with references to the North Atlantic Treaty and to the values and principles shared by Greece and the United States and ostensibly reflected in their security relationship (see appendix D).

CHAPTER 2

1. Ellen B. Laipson, "Cyprus: A Quarter Century of U.S. Policy," in John T. A. Koumoulides, ed., *Cyprus in Transition, 1960–1985* (London: Trigraph, 1986), p. 55.
2. To paraphrase the words of the former speaker of the House, Thomas P. (Tip) O'Neill.
3. The following account is based on notes kept by the author, who was then a member of the GTI staff and directly involved in the proceedings. It is worth recalling for what it shows of the limitations of foreign policy positions taken essentially for internal rather than external reasons and developed by bureaucratic rather than analytical processes.
4. Department of State Press Release No. 552, September 18, 1955.
5. *New York Times,* September 19, 1955, p. 1.
6. *Washington Post,* September 21, 1955, p. 10.

7. Papagos's reply to Dulles, as broadcast by Athens Radio medium-wave "Our Cyprus" service, September 21, 1955 (Foreign Broadcast Information Service [hereafter FBIS], September 23, 1955).

8. Menderes's reply to Dulles, as broadcast by the Turkish Home Service, September 21, 1955 (FBIS, September 22, 1955). The Turkish prime minister's reference to the "clandestine communist organization and leftist elements" was a particularly cynical Cold War touch, since one of the acts for which Menderes was hanged five years later was his own government's organization of the Istanbul and Izmir riots.

9. *New York Times*, September 24, 1955, p. 18.

10. See appendix A for the text of Dulles's letters.

11. See chapter 6 below.

12. Alexis Alexandris, *The Greek Minority of Istanbul and Greek-Turkish Relations, 1918–1974* (Athens: Center for Asia Minor Studies, 1983), p. 270.

13. *New York Times*, September 19, 1955, p. 11.

14. *Christian Science Monitor*, September 23, 1955, p. 1.

15. *Washington Post*, September 21, 1955, p. 10.

16. See appendix B for the text of Johnson's letter.

17. George W. Ball, *The Past Has Another Pattern* (New York: W.W. Norton, 1982), pp. 353–59.

18. Edward Weintal and Charles Bartlett, *Facing the Brink* (New York: Charles Scribner's Sons, 1967), p. 36, as quoted in Ball, *The Past Has Another Pattern*, p. 359.

19. Glafkos Clerides, *Cyprus: My Deposition*, vol. 2 (Athens: Alithia, 1989), pp. 112–14.

20. Ball, *The Past Has Another Pattern*, p. 359.

21. Here again, the letter shows signs of careless drafting. The final sentence would read more clearly if it ended, " . . . if Turkey *without the full consent and understanding of its NATO allies* takes a step which results in Soviet intervention."

22. Ball, *The Past Has Another Pattern*, p. 350.

23. Directorate of Intelligence, *Handbook of Economic Statistics*, Washington, D.C., 1987.

24. Ball, *The Past Has Another Pattern*, p. 350.

25. In February 1964, when there were press accounts of anti-American demonstrations in Athens and crowds burning Johnson's picture, Ball reports that the president telephoned him and expressed his concern. Ball comments, "Apart from injured feelings, he worried that such incidents might alienate the Greek-American vote in the forthcoming November elections" (*The Past Has Another Pattern*, p. 349).

CHAPTER 3

1. Which also pitted Greeks against inhabitants of what is now modern Turkey.

2. Section 620C(b)4 of the Foreign Service Act of 1961, as amended.

3. Active: 579,200 (498,800 conscripts); reserves: 1,107,000 to age 46 (all); army 470,000; navy 52,000; air force 57,200 (*The Military Balance 1990–1991* [London: International Institute for Strategic Studies, 1990]).

4. In 1980, the executive branch estimated that $3–4 billion would be needed over the ensuing five years (Senate Foreign Relations Committee, Staff Report, March 30, 1980: Turkey, Greece, and NATO: The Strained Alliance, p. 18). The actual appropriation was less than half that.

5. Unclassified telegram 636 from the U.S. embassy, Ankara, to the Department of State, January 15, 1988. Author's files.

6. FYs 1946–1948, 29:10; 1949, 19:10; 1950, 31:10; 1951, 19:10.

7. FYs 1952, 6:10; 1953, 8:10; 1954, 4:10; 1955, 3:10; 1956, 5:10; 1957, 4:10; 1958, 6:10; 1959, 4:10; 1960, 11:10; 1961, 5:10; 1962, 2:10; 1963, 4:10.

8. FYs 1964, 8:10; 1965, 9:10; 1966, 8:10.

9. FYs 1967, 4:10; 1968, 3:10; 1969, 5:10; 1970, 4:10; 1971, 5:10; 1972, 5:10; 1973, 3:10; 1974, 4:10.

10. FYs 1975, 8:10; 1976, no military aid to Turkey; 1977, 12:10; 1978, 10:10; 1979, 10:10 (although the Turkish arms embargo was in effect during FYs 1976–1979, "pipeline" aid continued, as well as other forms of assistance not requiring new appropriations. This accounts for Turkish figures nearly equal to Greek aid levels in the embargo years).

11. It is of passing interest that when the United States chooses to apply political criteria, Greece is more likely to be judged for internal lapses and Turkey for external ones. Thus, Greek military aid was docked after the Colonels' coup of 1967, but Turkish aid was not after the Generals' coup of 1980; and Turkey was penalized for intervening in Cyprus in 1974, but not Greece, either then or in 1964 or 1967. Perhaps this is no more than tacit recognition that political boundaries in Turkey can be as indistinct as territorial ones in Greece.

12. Principal items in the 1977 DECA package, such as the aid component and the Kissinger-Bitsios exchange, have been referred to publicly. The author, who was U.S. negotiator until the fall of 1976, is familiar with other provisions.

13. As we have seen, the failure of the executive branch to secure these amounts has caused dissatisfaction in Turkey. In March 1987, for example, the "best efforts" formula was reinforced in an exchange of letters, ratification of which was temporarily suspended by the Turks when aid for FY 1988 again fell below projected levels. Having made their protest, they finally ratified the extension in early 1988.

14. Dankwart A. Rustow, *Turkey: America's Forgotten Ally* (New York: Council on Foreign Relations, 1987). The title, incidentally, was not Professor Rustow's choice.

15. Turkey's population is over 51 million (growth rate, 2.5 percent); it has over 550,000 active duty military personnel; its land area is 296,000 square miles (about the size of Texas); it controls the Bosphorus and the Dardanelles and has a 380-mile border with the Soviet Union in the east and a Black Sea coast of 702 miles.

16. Greece's population is 10.2 million (with a near-zero growth rate); it has 158,500 active duty military personnel; its land area is 51,146 square miles

(about the size of Alabama); it shares borders of 300 miles with Bulgaria in the east, 200 miles with Yugoslavia, and 100 miles with Albania, and has over 2,000 strategically placed islands in the Aegean and eastern Mediterranean.

CHAPTER 4

1. The figure of 5 percent comes from Clyde Haberman, "Turks Claim Some of Victors' Spoils," *New York Times,* March 13, 1991, p. 14. Pentagon sources say that this estimate is conservative and does not take into account the fact that Turkey's proximity to Northern Iraq permitted sorties flown from Turkish bases to strike important targets outside the range of aircraft launched from more remote locations. The U.S. navy's total sortie rate is disputed, with some estimates placing it as low as 4 percent and others as high as 15 percent.
2. George McGhee, *Envoy to the Middle World* (New York: Harper & Row, 1983), pp. 265–76.
3. Bruce Kuniholm, "Rhetoric and Reality in the Aegean," *SAIS Review,* vol. 6 (Winter-Spring 1986), pp. 137–57.
4. Text of Gorbachev press conference held at the Soviet compound, Mt. Alto, in Washington, D.C., December 10, 1987 in *Federal News Service,* p. 14.
5. "Soviet Urges Naval Cuts in Mediterranean," *Washington Post,* March 17, 1988, p. 33.
6. The issue of Mersin and CFE zone continues to agitate Greek politics and the Greek press. The Greek government insists that the port is included in the CFE zone, contrary to the assertions of the Turkish government. The author is reliably informed that, among others, the United States *and* the Soviet Union have tabled letters of interpretation that support the Turkish position. Clearly, Mersin will continue to be an issue in Greek-Turkish-Cypriot relations, even if it is no longer one in CFE negotiations where, however, as late as December 1989, it was still being cited as a stumbling block in Vienna. See, for example, R. Jeffrey Smith, "Dispute Between Turkey, Greece Delaying Action on Treaty," *Washington Post,* November 23, 1989, p. A70.
7. On a visit to Cyprus in July 1990 the author was told by Communist party (AKEL) officials that it is the only Greek-Cypriot party organized on intercommunal lines.
8. Although the Soviets in 1945 and 1946 threatened to request revision of the Montreux Convention, the terms of which permit the signatories this option every ten years, they refrained from actually doing so. Nevertheless, it is doubtful that any Soviet leader today would use the words of the Soviet diplomatic historian, V. P. Potemkin, who described it in 1945 as "a great victory for Soviet diplomacy." See Harry N. Howard, *Turkey, the Straits and U.S. Policy* (Baltimore, Johns Hopkins University Press, 1974), p. 155n.
9. Only a month before he took the final decision to launch Operation Barbarossa, the attack on his Soviet ally that took place in June 1941.

10. Raymond James Sontag and James Stuart Bedie, eds., *Nazi-Soviet Relations, 1939–1941: Documents from the Archives of the German Foreign Office* (Westport, CT: Greenwood Press, 1976), p. 244.
11. Ibid., pp. 245–46.
12. Ibid., pp. 258–59.
13. Ibid., pp. 245–46.
14. Howard, *Turkey*, p. 234.
15. The word "apparent" is used because much of what passes for Greek unpredictability is actually angry submission to Greek reality in the form of limited resources, perilous location, and long coastline.
16. Milovan Djilas, *Conversations with Stalin* (Harmondsworth, Middlesex: Penguin Books Ltd., 1963) p. 140.
17. See appendix C.
18. Author's notes from Haig's Athens press conference, May 16, 1982.
19. See appendix D.
20. Duygu Bazoglu Sezer, "Turkey's Security Policies," in Jonathan Alford, ed., *Greece and Turkey: Adversity in Alliance*, International Institute for Strategic Studies (London: 1984), p. 74.
21. Jed C. Snyder, *Defending the Fringe* (Boulder, Col.: Westview Press and Johns Hopkins University Press, 1987), p. 46.
22. Lawrence S. Kaplan and Robert W. Clawson, "NATO and the Mediterranean Powers in Historical Perspective," in Lawrence S. Kaplan, Robert W. Clawson, and Raimondo Luraghi, eds., *NATO and the Mediterranean* (Wilmington, Del.: Scholarly Resources, 1985), p. 13.
23. Sergei G. Gorshkov, "Red Star Rising at Sea," trans. by Theodore A. Neely, Jr. (Annapolis: Naval Institute Press, 1974), p. 20.
24. Figures on Soviet Mediterranean ship days are drawn from Mariano Gabriele, "Mediterranean Naval Forces," in Kaplan, Clawson, and Luraghi, eds., *NATO*, p. 69, and Gordon McCormick, *Soviet Strategic Aims and Capabilities in the Mediterranean*, Adelphi Paper No. 229, Part II (London: International Institute for Strategic Studies, Spring 1988), p. 36. Data on the Fifth Eskadra's unit deployments come from Laurence Martin, *NATO and the Defense of the West* (New York: Holt, Rinehart & Winston, 1985), p. 34. Information on reduced Soviet fleet exercises appears in Michael R. Gordon, "Soviets Scale Back Naval Deployments and Large Exercises," *New York Times*, July 17, 1988. p. 1. The estimate of Soviet fleet deployments during the gulf crisis comes from U.S. government sources.

CHAPTER 5

1. Dimitri Bitsios, *Pera Apo Ta Synora* (Athens: Estia Press, 1982), p. 204.
2. The air-space dispute between Greece and Turkey is examined in more detail in chapter 9.
3. See chapter 9.
4. The commander in chief at the time was Adm. William Crowe, later to become chairman of the U.S. Joint Chiefs of Staff.
5. This "solution" to the Limnos problem was strikingly similar to that proposed five years later to resolve the Mersin deadlock (chapter 4, above).

6. For a recent discussion of Greek and Turkish defense doctrines and battles, see Robert McDonald, "Alliance Problems in Eastern Mediterranean," Part II, Aldelphi Paper No. 229, Part I (London: International Institute for Strategic Studies, Spring 1988). McDonald notes significant Greek and Turkish troop deployments unrelated to NATO planning, including up to 30,000 Greek troops in eastern Aegean islands and between 30,000 (Turkish estimate) and 150,000 (Greek estimate) Turkish troops facing them in the Turkish Fourth Army created in 1975.
7. Aide-mémoire from Ambassador Gifford and NAC Deputy Representative Spofford to Strang, May 15, 1951, *Foreign Relations of the United States, 1951*, Vol. III, pp. 520–22.
8. At the U.S. embassy in Ankara, where the author was serving in the summer of 1950, the military threat to Turkey was thought to be so grave after the outbreak of the Korean War that an evacuation plan for U.S. residents was prepared, and a handful of officials were designated to remain behind in the event of a Soviet occupation of Ankara.
9. Telegram from U.S. ambassador in Greece (Peurifoy) to secretary of state, National Archives: 740.5/8-3151.
10. Nicholas Henderson, *The Birth of NATO* (Boulder, Col.: Westview Press, 1983), gives an excellent firsthand account of the meetings of the Working Group.
11. Henderson, *Birth of NATO*, pp. 71–72.
12. Ibid., p. 104.
13. George W. Ball in *The Past Has Another Pattern* details Washington's reaction to the Cyprus crisis of 1964, pp. 337–59.
14. See chapter 1.
15. Adelphi Paper No. 155 (London: International Institute for Strategic Studies, Winter 1979/1980).

CHAPTER 6

1. The questions of conflicting claims to territorial sea and shelf in the Aegean are more complicated and will be dealt with in greater detail in chapter 9.
2. Treaty of Guarantee, signed and initialed at Lancaster House, London, February 19, 1959, by representatives of Greece, Turkey, and the United Kingdom.
3. See Sir David Hunt's discussion of this issue, "Three Greek Islands and the Development of International Law," in Koumoulides, ed., *Cyprus in Transition*, pp. 44–50.
4. United Nations Charter, Article 2(4).
5. Iphigenia Anastasiadou, *O Venizelos kai to Ellenoturkiko Symphono Filias tou 1930* (Venizelos and the Greek-Turkish Treaty of Friendship of 1930) [Athens: Filippoti Editions, 1982], p. 13 (author's translation).
6. Ibid.
7. Ibid., p. 14.
8. Ibid., p. 15.

9. Iphigenia Anastasiadou, "Venizelos and the Greek-Turkish Treaty of Friendship of 1930," in O. Dimitrakopoulos and T. Veremis, eds., *Meletimata Yuro Apo Ton Venizelos Kai tin Epohki Tou* (Studies on Venizelos and his times) [Athens: Filippoti Editions, 1980] p. 395, n. 12 (author's translation).

10. Anastasiadou, *O Venizelos*, p. 16.

11. Ibid., pp. 66–67.

12. Ibid., p. 66.

13. The Seljuk Turks appeared in Eastern Anatolia in the eleventh century A.D.

14. *Roumeli: Travels in Northern Greece* (London: John Murray, 1966) pp. 98–99n.

15. For a description of Greek-Turkish coexistence at the village level in colonial Cyprus—guarded and compartmentalized but peaceful—see Lawrence Durrell, *Bitter Lemons* (New York: E.P. Dutton, 1957).

16. A reminder of this has appeared at the time of this writing. The Greek government in February 1991 strongly protested references in the State Department's annual human rights report for 1990 to a "nonexistent Slavo-Macedonian minority" in Greece.

17. For excellent contrasting—but not always contradictory—views of the minorities question, one Greek, the other Turkish, see Alexis Alexandris's *Greek Minority of Istanbul and Greek-Turkish Relations* and Tozun Bahceli, *Greek-Turkish Relations Since 1955* (Boulder, Col.: Westview Press, 1990), chapter 6 of which is titled "Irritants Over the Treatment of Minorities."

CHAPTER 7

1. *Threat in the Aegean.* The Journalists' Union of the Athens Daily Newspapers, undated, but probably published in 1985.

2. *The Aegean Realities.* Association of Journalists, Gazeteciler Cemyeti, Basin Sarayi, Cagaloglu, Istanbul, undated, but probably published in 1986.

3. Turkish per capita GNP (1990): $2,000; Greek per capita GNP (1990): $6,600 (*The Military Balance*, 1991–1992 [London: International Institute for Strategic Studies, 1991]).

4. Estimated at 2,200 men, with standing instructions to use arms only in self-defense. See Andrew Borowiec, *The Mediterranean Feud* (New York: Praeger, 1983), p. 90 and Koumoulides, ed., *Cyprus in Transition*, p. 47.

5. As quoted in *Athens News*, April 23–24, 1989, p. 3.

6. See appendix C.

7. Quotations from the preamble to the 1990 DCA are from *Greece's Weekly*, July 16, 1990. For the full text of the preamble, see appendix D.

8. For a Turkish account of Ankara's reaction to the DCA, see the *Turkish Daily News*, June 30–July 1, 1990.

9. Who was attending the Brussels meeting not as premier but in his dual capacity as defense minister.

10. See Harold Nicholson, *Diplomacy* (London: Oxford University Press, 1952), p. 237.

11. See James Callaghan, *Time and Chance* (London: Collins/Fontana, 1988), pp. 331–58.
12. See chapter 5, pp. 78–79.
13. See, for example, "An Incident Worsens Greek-Turkish Ties," *New York Times*, January 14, 1989, p. 2.
14. Report of the North Atlantic Council on the Future Tasks of the Alliance (Harmel Report), Annex to the Final Communiqué of the Ministerial Meeting, December, 1967, quoted in Lawrence S. Kaplan, *NATO and the United States: The Enduring Alliance* (Boston: Twayne Publishers, 1988), p. 223.

CHAPTER 8

1. The figures used by Robert McDonald in his monograph *The Problem of Cyprus*, Aldephi Papers 234 (London: International Institute for Strategic Studies, Winter 1988/89). Since 1974, a significant number of Turkish settlers have moved to northern Cyprus with the encouragement of Ankara and Turkish Cypriot authorities. Estimates range between 40,000 and 60,000. In the same period, an indeterminate number of Turkish Cypriots have left the island, so the exact effect of immigration from Anatolia on the population balance in Cyprus is unclear. McDonald notes that both Athens and Ankara have charged each other with attempts to alter the population balance. In the absence of a new, island-wide census, the 80:18 ratio remains the best available estimate.
2. Professor Biron Yesilada of the University of Missouri pointed out in a letter to the author that "the 1960 political framework of Cyprus was a unique form of unitary state. It was based on the principles of consociational democracy. It is useful to note the elements of this system because the Greek-Cypriots, from time to time since 1974, have proposed a return to a similar political order. It is not acceptable to the Turkish-Cypriots." For the purposes of this study, it is probably sufficient to note that by a "unitary" state the author means a state with a central government conducting foreign and military affairs on behalf of all its citizens and conducting internal affairs as regulated by a single constitution.
3. The flag has its defenders. In the summer of 1990, the president of the National Assembly of the Republic of Cyprus, Glafkos Clerides, told the author that the flag of Cyprus is "the best in the world." When asked why, he replied, "Because no one would die for it."
4. These, and the following figures for the Republic of Cyprus, were obtained in discussions with Cypriot and U.S. embassy officials on a visit to Cyprus in July 1990.
5. See chapter 1, above.
6. Grivas's first return to Cyprus after it became independent in 1960 was in 1964, following the outbreak of intercommunal violence in December 1963.
7. McDonald, *The Problem of Cyprus*, pp. 16–17.
8. See, for example, C. M. Woodhouse, *The Rise and Fall of the Greek Colonels* (New York: Franklin Watts, 1985), chapters 7 and 8.

9. Zaim M. Necatigil, *The Cyprus Question and the Turkish Position in International Law* (Oxford: Oxford University Press, 1989), p. 70.

10. Clerides reaffirmed to the author (in the summer of 1990) that he and Denktash had reached substantial agreement on the elements of a settlement, which Clerides had recommended that the government of Cyprus accept. Clerides also agreed on the reasons why Archbishop Makarios had declined to accept his recommendation (see below).

11. William S. Shepard, "The Cyprus Issue: Waiting for Sadat," in Nikolaos A. Stavrou, ed., *Greece Under Socialism* (New Rochelle, N.Y.: Orpheus Publishing, Inc., 1988), p. 402, n. 25.

12. The Treaty of Friendship, Non-Aggression and Arbitration, signed by Ataturk and Venizelos in 1930 and referred to in chapter 6, would not have been possible had the more complex and comprehensive Treaty of Lausanne not preceded it.

13. Named after the hotel on the Nicosia Green Line where they took place under UN auspices.

14. *American Diplomacy in Turkey* (New York: Praeger, 1984), pp. 49–57.

15. Ibid., p. 54.

16. Brian Urquhart, *A Life in Peace and War* (New York: Harper & Row, 1987), p. 198.

17. A position, we were told elsewhere, that the Turkish military commander, General Bitlis, does not share. Referring to the Turkish troop presence, Denktash indicated that reductions in their number would be possible without imperiling Turkish Cypriot security. Such a decision would, of course, have to be taken in Ankara.

18. Opening statement delivered by Secretary General Pérez de Cuéllar on February 26, 1990 (Secretary Council document S/21183, Annex I, February 26, 1990, pp. 6–11).

19. Mary Anne Weaver estimates the annual cost of Cyprus peacekeeping to be $100 million and says the total bill reached over two billion in 1989 ("Report from Cyprus" *New Yorker,* April 6, 1990).

20. As this manuscript is being completed, it is still too early to judge whether President Bush's official visits to Greece and Turkey, July 18–22, 1991, will produce movement toward the solution of the Cyprus problem and an improved climate of Greek-Turkish relations. Such visits have the virtue of focusing the attention of senior U.S. officials on problems that do not regularly receive their attention, and the president has expressed himself as optimistic that a Cyprus settlement can be achieved before the end of 1991. We can hope his optimism to be justified while bearing in mind the complexity of the issue, the effect on Cyprus of unresolved bilateral Greek-Turkish problems, and the need for patient diplomatic follow-through after the speeches have been made, the toasts exchanged, and the wreaths laid in Athens and Ankara.

21. FBIS monitors and transcribes in English foreign international broadcasts. It is an unclassified service under administrative control of the Central Intelligence Agency.

22. By Public Law 95-384.

23. The Department of Defense announced in March 1990 its intention to close Nea Makri, along with Hellinikon Air Force Base, as part of a general overseas bases retrenchment.
24. From text of letter from the president to the speaker of the House of Representatives and the chairman of the Committee on Foreign Relations. White House Press Release, April 21, 1987.
25. Urquhart, *Life in Peace and War,* p. 259.
26. Sezer, "Turkey's Security Policies," in Alford, ed., *Greece and Turkey.*

CHAPTER 9

1. It would be hard to identify terrain features anywhere in the world that have exercised so decisive a strategic influence for so long a time as the Bosphorus and the Dardanelles, both controlled by Turkey. Some scholars argue that the Trojan Wars were less likely to have been fought over the beautiful Helen than over control of the grain trade from the Crimea.
2. The Great Lakes cover 95,000 sq. miles.
3. This is not only a military or military-support function. Shortly after the crisis erupted, President Bush was quoted as saying that Greece and Turkey were involved "in an awful lot of diplomacy behind the scenes," presumably in developing support for the quarantining of Iraq (*New York Times,* August 23, 1990, p. A17).
4. Since 1974, there have been two serious episodes: one in July and August of 1976, when a Turkish vessel, *Hora* (later renamed *Sismik I* by the Turks), undertook to conduct seismic soundings in a disputed area of the shelf; the other in March 1987, when Ankara gained the impression that the Greek government intended to conduct petroleum exploration eleven miles east of the northern Greek island of Thasos in an area outside Greek territorial waters.
5. The Bern Declaration resulted from an effort by the Greek and Turkish governments to give effect to UN Security Council Resolution 395 of August 25, 1976, which called on them to engage in direct negotiations to resolve their differences but urged them not to forget that the International Court was available to assist them in settling differences they could not resolve bilaterally. The wording was carefully drafted by NATO allies of Greece and Turkey to allow both to support it. Resolution 395 does not therefore provide clear guidance on procedures to be followed in the shelf dispute. Turkey can point to the reference to direct talks as endorsement of its position, and Greece to the reference to the court. Opposition leaders in both countries have denounced the declaration as unacceptably compromising to national interests.
6. See note 5 above.
7. *Aegean Realities,* p. 31.
8. *Threat in the Aegean,* p. 20.
9. As noted in chapter 5.
10. The "Contiguous Zone" defined by the 1958 convention has been interpreted by many states as permitting them to extend their territorial sea boundaries to twelve miles. Turkey has done so in the Black Sea and the

Mediterranean but notes that the convention is not mandatory and argues that it does not apply to a semi-enclosed sea like the Aegean.

11. These percentages are taken from Andrew Wilson's excellent study, "The Aegean Dispute," in Alford, ed., *Greece and Turkey: Adversity in Alliance*. The Turkish government, in its previously cited publication, *Aegean Realities*, gives slightly different figures: for six miles, 43.5 percent Greek, 7.5 percent Turkish, and 49 percent high seas; for twelve miles, 71.5 percent Greek, 8.8 percent Turkish, and 19.7 percent high seas.

12. See chapter 5.

13. Wilson gives a clear resumé of how these treaties prescribe, in varying degrees, permissible levels of military preparedness for the Aegean islands. He also notes the Greek argument that the important islands of Limnos and Samothraki, which had been demilitarized by the Treaty of Lausanne in 1923, were exempted from this constraint by the Montreux Convention in 1936 and that this fact was officially acknowledged at the time by the Turkish foreign minister.

CHAPTER 10

1. Cuba might be cited as another, except that the United States was granted, by an agreement with the Cuban government signed in 1903 and renewed in 1934, a lease on the 28,000-acre naval station in Guantanamo that could not be revoked without its consent. No such agreement covers the Turkish military presence in Cyprus, although the Turkish government contends that its intervention—and therefore, by extension, its continued presence—in Cyprus is authorized by the 1960 Treaty of Guarantee until "the state of affairs created by the present treaty" is reestablished (Article Four of the Treaty of Guarantee). The Turkish case is weakened by the fact that both the Turks and the Turkish Cypriots have made clear that reestablishment of the state of affairs created by the Zurich and London accords is exactly what they regard as unacceptable. As noted in chapter 8, the Turkish interpretation of Article Four is disputed by the governments of Greece and the Republic of Cyprus and has not found favor in a series of UN resolutions calling for the withdrawal of foreign troops from Cyprus.

2. The financing of this force is provided on a voluntary basis by the troop-contributing countries, rather than by an assessment levied on all members. This arrangement is understandably resented by the troop contributors and the wherewithal to maintain the UN force indefinitely, in the absence of a settlement, cannot be taken for granted.

3. Section XII reads: "Notwithstanding a request by a party under either Section IV or Section XI, the [settlement] Mechanism will not be established or continued, as the case may be, if another party to the dispute considers that because the dispute raises issues concerning its territorial integrity, or national defense, title to sovereignty over land territory, or competing claims with regard to the jurisdiction over other areas, the Mechanism should not be established or continued" (*Report of the CSCE Meeting of Experts on Peaceful Settlement of Disputes, Valletta 1991*). The Greeks and Turks had different interpretations of the phrase "or compet-

ing claims with regard to the jurisdiction over other areas" and made separate statements to that effect.

4. Alastair Buchan Memorial Lecture, delivered at the International Institute for Strategic Studies, London, March 7, 1991.

5. See, for example, Richard N. Haass, *Conflicts Unending: The United States and Regional Disputes* (New Haven: Yale University Press, 1990), pp. 57–77.

6. President Truman's address before a joint session of Congress, March 12, 1947.

7. Leaving aside the British military presence in the sovereign base areas, the largest foreign military mission in Cyprus is France's.

8. The author is indebted to Professor Harry Psomiades of Queens College, New York, who supplied figures on Greek inhabitants of the Soviet Union, drawn from the 1977 Soviet census, which further specifies that, of the total of 325,000 Greeks in the USSR, 130,000 are Greek-speaking and 195,000 are Russian-speaking. The majority reside in the Pontic regions on the eastern coast of the Black Sea. Professor Psomiades believes the total given by the Soviet census to be on the low side. He also estimates that about 50,000 Soviet Greeks have been resettled in Greece in the past few years.

INDEX